A Moss-Covered Trail
A Walk Across the Ozark Highlands

By

Matt Dunn

A MOSS-COVERED TRAIL. Copyright © 2016 by Matt Dunn. All rights reserved. No part of this book may be used or reproduced in any manner whatsoever without written permission except in the case of brief quotations embodied in critical articles and reviews.

ISBN 978-15397554114

Introduction

The Ozark Highlands Trail began as an idea in the mind of photographer and native Arkansawyer Tim Ernst. With a backpack, some maps, and plenty of determination he pioneered much of the route of the original 165-mile trail. In addition, he literally wrote the book on it, which I used as the guidebook for my thru-hike.

A thru-hike is considered a hike of the entire length of a trail, be it the Appalachian Trail, Continental Divide Trail, or in this case, the Ozark Highlands Trail. The original route, as I call it, was from Lake Fort Smith State Park in western Arkansas to Woolum on the Buffalo National River in north Arkansas. In the years before my thru-hike, Lake Fort Smith had been enlarged, closing down the westernmost 6 miles of the trail. It was only in the spring of 2008, the year I hiked it, that the trail once again had an official western terminus. Thus, I had the good fortune to be among the first to thru-hike the new version of the trail.

Additionally, at the time I hiked plans to extend the

eastern terminus were being considered. In anticipation of that extension, I hiked past Woolum, the then-current terminus, on the Buffalo River Trail to Tyler Bend and Highway 65, making for a total of 180 continuous miles.

The trail is broken up into 8 sections, 7 of them roughly 20 miles and 1 of them about 30 miles. I hiked these sections over a number a years before my thru-hike, which is reflected in the following account.

As with most accounts of hiking, you'll notice a preoccupation with food and gear weight. I find it is truer to the experience to leave those thoughts in and risk the chance of seeming repetitive. Anyone who's spent much time hiking and backpacking can relate.

Lastly, if you'd like to visually follow along on my travels, I've posted many photos from my hike here: https://www.flickr.com/photos/139304774@N04/albums/72157660946621944.

Dedication

To those who planned, built, and maintain the trail,

and

to those with whom I've walked it.

1

In the autumn I decided to take a walk.

The walk I chose was a continuous journey across the Ozark Highlands of my native state. It was a walk I'd already done in short sections, but I'd never done it all at once. For years I had wanted to do just that, but work and other circumstances had thus far prevented me from doing so. Until now.

The night before the start, I check and re-check my gear several times until I'm satisfied I have everything. For good measure I add a few more snacks to the top pouch of my backpack, for extra energy on my first day.

With everything inside, I lift the pack and hang it on a handheld scale. The needle settles exactly the at the 40 pound line, including water. All the provisions inside have to last me seven days and just over eighty miles until I reach my resupply point near the halfway point of the 180 mile walk.

While I'm weighing things, I step on the bathroom scale to see that I'm about 150 lbs. That's down from my strongest weight of 155, and somehow I still have a bit of a belly.

As if the anxiety and anticipation weren't enough to keep me awake during the night, the loud and ominous patter of rain and disheartening gusts of wind conspire to make sleep difficult. My last shower has left me smelling the best I will for the next two weeks or so, and my bed seems far more luxurious than usual. Still, sleep comes only in short stretches.

I am deeply asleep when my alarm goes off at six o'clock, but adrenaline quickly gets me up and moving. The first light of day is barely beginning to show, filtered through the heavy, wet clouds that are hanging low in the sky. Not ideal weather, but because I can't do anything to change the weather, I get dressed and ready. No use wasting time when I hope to do at least ten miles today, and I'm not even at the trailhead yet. I'm too nervous to even think about making the big pancake breakfast I'd imagined, so I drink several cups of tea, eat some shredded wheat cereal, and have a glass of orange juice.

My folks graciously drive me to the trailhead at Lake Fort Smith State Park, about half an hour away. Despite the low clouds the views along Highway 71 are beautiful: long, dark ridges of barren hardwood trees sloping away on both sides of the roadway. Wisps of fog hang in the sheltered valleys.

The lake itself is the reservoir of drinking water for my hometown. It has been enlarged in recent years, and as we drive down the new park entrance road to the visitor center, I see it for the first time. The expansion of the lake flooded the first six original miles of the Trail, which ran along the east side. The new section of trail now starts on the west side of the lake, and winds around the north side, crossing Frog Bayou (the feeder stream to the lake) to tie into the rest of the trail.

There's only one car in the parking lot as we pull into the visitor center, and no sign of any other hikers. A dreary weekday morning in the fall at a state park is obviously not the best place to find people, a fact for which I am glad.

The trailhead is easy to find: a large and beautiful wooden sign, carved with sylvan scenes, marks the beginning. I pose for pictures beside the sign, then hug my parents good-bye. The air is completely silent but for our words. I turn down the sidewalk towards the lake and the rest of the trail. The excitement within in me is scarcely containable.

It is November 11, 2008, about a quarter to nine o'clock, as I set off into the woods. These first five or six miles, as well as the last fifteen, are the only parts of the trail that I have not hiked before, though it has been more than two years since I have hiked any section of it.

The first miles are marked with plastic silver arrows in white circles, unlike the standard two-by-six painted white blazes that mark the route of the rest of the trail. The new markers are also placed quite frequently along the trail, with four or five in sight at any time, also unlike the rest of trail.

Much of the first mile is just below the park campground, which appears vacant. I had not realized it was so big: ten minutes of walking and I glimpse a lone RV incongruously parked amongst the trees.

The trail ambles and undulates up and around the west and north shore of the lake, with pleasant views out across the cool, smooth surface of the water. Soon I find myself at mile marker 1. Only 179 to go.

As with any long-distance hike, one of the primary concerns is water, both crossing and drinking. In regards to the former, there are numerous wet crossings ahead today, undoubtedly swollen by the overnight rain. On top of that, it was a wet summer in the area and the reservoir sure looks full. The first water crossing, Frog Bayou, is several miles ahead. There is the possibility that I might have to make a major detour or turn back entirely if it is not crossable.

According to the morning weather, it has rained about an inch since yesterday morning. That's a lot of water, which makes me worry about the crossings. There's no telling how high the creeks might be flowing. On the flip side, the rain will help by keeping the smaller streams flush with water. This is key because I'm only carrying one 27 ounce water bottle, with a collapsed two-liter bottle for reserve. Weight and space considerations deter me from hiking with it full.

Because I'm a ways out from any creeks, I try not to

worry and enjoy the walk. As the trail joins an old roadbed near the lakeshore, I catch a glimpse of a large moving object in the trees up and to my right. The six-foot wingspan, brown body, and white-tipped head and tail are unmistakeable: Bald Eagle. It swoops gracefully from an oak and heads out over the lake. I stand and watch it through the trees until it flies behind a tree-covered bend of the lakeshore. I've never seen one so close, nor seen one at all in Arkansas. I take it as a good omen for my journey.

After following a narrow arm of the lake, I hear a creek ahead: Frog Bayou. We are no strangers to one another: I floated a section of it as a boy (one of my early memories) and even lived beside it several winters previous. I grew up drinking its water.

My worry about the water level fades as it comes into view. It looks like I can rock hop across without having to take the boots off and dip my feet in the frigid water. I find a wide, shallow spot and splash across the stream to the woods on the other side. For some reason, there is an excessive amount of flagging hanging on the other side: I count nine different colored pieces on one bush, and several more on the leaves underneath.

Here I see the white blazes. No more silver arrows. The trail swings back and forth into the woods and back towards the lakeshore. The walking is easy and pleasant. The woods are lovely and deep here, but not dark. Nary a tree but the beeches have any leaves on them (beeches keep their leaves all year round). Only birds and moss are in the trees this time of year. Even with an overcast sky, the forest here feels open, and the air crisp and fresh.

Further on I flush a pair of whitetail deer, a buck and a doe. Rifle season started the Friday before, so all three of us are a bit skittish. I take it as a sign that I should strap the hunter orange vest over my pack for visibility. I've already heard one gunshot boom and echo across the hills, and don't want to be close to another. I have run into hunters out on the trail before, and have found them to be a friendly, if luckless, bunch. I still have yet to meet one flush with the victory of a kill. Usually we talk a bit, shrug and smile as we part. I expect to meet a few on this trip.

So far I estimate that I've gone about four miles, despite the official mileage figure of five and a half. I'm now in the

Jack Creek drainage, which I will follow for the next five or so miles to Dockerys Gap. A short ways up the creek I reach a place that holds vivid memories for me from more than five years ago.

At that time I hadn't been to this area, so I hiked and camped around here for two days in late winter, just before spring. My sister was very pregnant at the time, but she had assured me that it would be another week before the doctors would induce labor. So naturally I headed to the woods to enjoy the pleasant weather and see some new country.

On the second afternoon out I took a long lunch near here. With my feet soaking in the cool water I snacked on cheese and crackers and basked in the sunshine. It was idyllic. After a long rest there I walked back to my truck and headed to my cabin on Frog Bayou. When I got there several phone messages awaited me, and even before listening I knew what they were. After I reached her by phone, she told me that my nephew had been born early that afternoon, at the same time I'd been lazing here, beside Jack Creek.

The situation is quite different now, but the memory cheers me. For now I'm just glad it's not raining. Before I left the house this morning I put on my rain pants, which seems to be keeping the rain at bay.

Soon I pass another mile marker, a brown carsonite post with a 6 sticker on it. Along with the white blazes these posts are the trail markers. Occasionally there are numbered diamonds nailed to trees for the mile markers, which I like the best.

The walking is not that taxing so far, though after the relative flat lakeside walk every little climb here is noticeable. I wind my way along the trail up and down through several rock benches and down into and up out of several tributaries of Jack Creek. The climb up to Dockerys Gap, a low spot on the ridge ahead, is a grunt, but I hike slow and steady to keep from burning out so early in the day. It is now noon, and according to the trail guide I've come nearly ten and a half miles. That boosts my confidence, but I know the miles ahead will be tougher than the ones behind.

The trail steeply descends from the gap down into Hurricane Creek. I've hiked it from the other direction with a full pack for exercise, and it worked me over. Going down now is a similar story, but for different reasons. The rain has made the rocky, leaf-covered trail slick, so it is a constant battle to keep my footing and prevent a nasty fall. One short slip on to my left side hurts, but makes me more cautious. The soreness in my legs tells me I should've stretched before I set out this morning.

No doubt I am pleased to see the trail bottom out after negotiating my way down the switchbacks. My stomach has been growling the whole way down, so I hop the rocks across Hurricane Creek and have lunch on the other side. On the menu is a 1.5 oz packet of peanut butter and with a couple of fig newtons, followed by a handful of my personal trail mix (Reese's Pieces and M&Ms) for dessert. The cool air in the creek bottom keeps me from lingering.

After eating I start up the east side of Hurricane Creek, the first of two such named creeks of the walk. It is the second one that I am very much looking forward to, but first I have to get there.

Before lunch I'd planned on tanking up on all the water I could carry and find a campsite for the night just up the hill. But now, feeling energized from lunch, I feel like I can keep going for another couple of hours.

The next reliable, year-round creek is nearly ten miles away, so I'm hoping the rain has filled a few of the smaller streambeds between here and there. Vague memories from earlier hikes in the area make me think there are some possibilities, so I'll see.

From here the trail leaves the drainages and follows a sloping ridgeline up towards White Rock Mountain, one of the most scenic places in the state. But on an overcast day like this one there is little to see.

From my previous experiences hiking in the fog, I can't say a whole lot to recommend it. Perhaps it is my own claustrophobia, or the feeling of being swallowed up in the clouds and unable to see any landmarks (or anything at all, for that matter) that makes me dread it. The one positive is that keeps other people inside, so at least I have the trail to myself.

Other people, except for the hunters. Coming to a forest road I pass near one of dozens, or even hundreds, of deer camps in these mountains. Here, Chevy trucks, old campers, and four-wheelers stand grouped together in a small clearing around a pleasant-smelling campfire. Several orange- and camouflage-clad men stand around talking and planning, no doubt telling old war stories and hoping for the weather to clear. One of the younger men sees me passing near and gives me a friendly wave. As I approach closer he asks if I've seen any whitetails, but I honestly tell him that I have not. He smiles and with another friendly wave sends me on my way. Scarcely a hundred yards down the trail all signs of the camp are gone in the fog.

Feeling a bit low on energy I take out a packet of Emergen-C and pour it in my mouth, along with a big swallow of water. A few minutes later I can feel the vitamins working: a warm sensation spreads from my belly to the rest of my body. The fog in my head seems to lift, and I notice that I'm running low on water. I stop and check my guidebook, then head on to the next dirt road. If nothing else, I figure there might be standing water along the road.

Just down the way is the head of a drainage that might hold water, so I walk that direction. A couple of hundred yards later I hear the unmistakeable sound of falling water, and see a small creekbed off the road. I make my way down the rain-slicked rocks and leaves to a small drop-off, where small rivulets of water run clear, cold, and plentiful.

When the water bottle is full, I drop some iodine tablets in and head back to the trail. It takes a half hour for the tablets to do their work, so I take note of the time as I walk along.

Besides the hunters' camp and the gunshots early on,

I've hardly seen or heard any human presence at all in these woods. This area is not official wilderness—I've crossed several roads today and will cross more before I stop—but it certainly feels wild. Out here humankind is more background noise than anything else. Just a passing presence, like myself.

So on I go. As I hike, the inevitable music starts up in my head. When people ask me what I think about when I hike, I tell them I have a head full of music. Of course I do a lot of thinking and reflecting, but the rhythm of walking always starts the stereo in my head. Usually I'll just hum or sing whatever comes to my head, but if I'm feeling especially ambitious, I'll try to go through a whole album. Once, on a hike in Ecuador in very similar conditions to these, I tried to go through Led Zeppelin's entire catalogue. It was the only thing I could do to stay sane.

As I walk on the fog thickens, becoming just short of oppressive. As compensation, I don't recall there being any views in this area, just the typical Southern hardwood forest with its black, white, and red oaks, black and sweet gums, hickories, maples, dogwoods, and many more that I don't know. Unfortunately this area has been hit hard in the previous years by a small yet devastating insect known as the red oak borer. It has killed thousands of acres of those noble old trees, leaving thousands of barren, barkless branches reaching desperately up to the indifferent sky.

Feeling another low come on, I stop at the next mile marker and take off my pack. It has been several hours and miles since lunch, so I reach into my pack and find some fig newtons. To savor it, I bite off half and slowly chew it. I'm sure I can taste every sweet ingredient, so I take my time with second half. If it tastes this good on the first day, I can only imagine how good one will taste a week from now, long after I've had any fresh food.

    After my snack break I pick up an old roadbed that makes for easy walking. I know that I will soon pass another potential water source at one of the bends in the trail, and thankfully I find that my memory was right. On the left side of the trail, beautiful lines of spring water drip off the barren sandstone. After I refill my bottle and add the iodine tabs I move on. Despite the cool weather I am trying to drink plenty of water, as I've found that these days I slack off on hydration and feel bad the next day.

    Along with the iodine tabs, I have my trusted water

filter along as a backup. I plan on using the iodine during the day, as it is quick and easy, and I'll use the filter in the evenings for drinking and cooking water.

With such a reliable water source and the afternoon hour, I decide to fill up the two-liter bottle here as well, in case I find a good camp spot. It's nearly three-thirty, which leaves me perhaps two hours of daylight to find a place to camp. And I prefer getting into camp when it is still light, especially on dreary days such as this.

Near mile marker 15 I see some potential sites below the trail and head off into the underbrush to take a look. Up close the sites don't look suitable, so I head back up to the trail. Emerging from the fog is a figure—another hiker, heading west and straight for me.

When I'd cached my food at my resupply point several days earlier, I checked the trail register nearby. I was pleased to see that there was one long distance hiker from Louisiana who, according to his card, was hiking to a campground 144 miles in, and instead of finishing the trail proper, would backtrack to his starting point. And he was taking a month to do it. Even before I met him, I liked him for undertaking such an adventure. Looking at the dates on the card, I figured I would likely meet him.

The approaching figure is wearing a purple and yellow beanie, which I recognize as the colors of Louisiana State University. *This has to be the guy*, I think. As he comes closer, I'm surprised at the large size of his pack: he isn't just backpacking—he's on an expedition.

He greets me with a handshake as we stop in front of each other. I ask if he is Lucas Boudreaux, the name I'd seen on the card several days earlier. He pauses and looks at me for several long seconds.

"Yes, I am," he says with a confused smile.

I told him how I'd seen his registration card and once I saw the beanie, figured it was him. He laughs, and I ask him how his hike is going. As he launches into his story, I can tell by his enthusiasm that he's glad to have human contact. And there's nothing like a Southerner to tell a good story.

Among other things, he'd had a bear at a campsite one night, had gone ten miles out of his way to get a sandwich several days before, and had a particularly difficult time on the east side of White Rock, due to all the deadfall he'd had to climb over. He also said he'd been cold the past several nights, despite the fleece blanket he had with him. But he still has the good spirits of one who is almost finished with a long ordeal, and he shakes my hand strongly as he wishes me good luck with my own hike. I turn back a few times to watch until he fades from view, and wonder when I'll see the next hiker.

Further on at the 16 mile point, I see some flat ground below the trail. Once again I crash through the wet underbrush to check it out. As I get closer I see evidence of others camping here. An old fire ring stand in the middle of some flat ground, with some long sittin' logs arranged beside it. Relieved, I take off my pack and begin my camp chores.

Camp chore number one is to set up my tarp. In order to save weight, I opted to carry a six-ounce waterproof tarp instead of three-pound tent. It typically doesn't get too cold this time of year here, and I figured that along with the tarp a lightweight bivy sack (another couple of ounces) would suffice to keep me dry on wet nights.

With my sleeping arrangements made, I lay down on my sleeping pad and devour a protein bar as an afternoon snack. I also make some tea to warm me and wake me up, but it doesn't work. After trying to read for a bit I start falling off to sleep. Thus I take my first nap of the trip.

The sun sets about five-thirty this time of year, and rises about seven, making for long nights. To make them pass a bit faster, I brought along Dostoyevsky's *The Brothers Karamazov*. Though I'm a weight-conscious backpacker, I usually make exceptions for reading material. This book, at a hefty 934 paperback pages, was a big one. In addition to my goal of 15 miles a day, I've added a reading requirement of 80 pages a night, which should last me 12 nights if I stay on schedule. But the mileage and reading are just averages. My main goal is just to enjoy myself.

As night comes on, so does the rain. It is light but steady. My tarp is keeping everything dry so far, so I set up the stove towards the high end to cook supper. Tonight it will be a double portion of noodles.

To save weight and stay organized, I put each evening meal in a quart-size plastic bag and added the powdered sauce, as well as powdered milk. The latter is both a substitute for the real thing and a source of extra calories. Thus all I need to do is dump the contents into four boiling quarts of water for a few minutes and I have a huge, hot, tasty supper. I open tonight's bag and catch a tantalizing whiff of garlic.

After adding the noodles to the steaming aluminum pot, I stir it to keep the noodles from sticking to bottom and burning. Because the stove burns so hot, stirring also keeps the pot from boiling over onto the small heat reflector I'd placed under the stove. The steam rising from the pot is strong and tempting, and my stomach responds with a vigorous round of growling. The only other sounds out here right now are the soft drops of light rain and the gentle rumble of the pasta and water in the pot.

At ten minutes the noodles are sufficiently cooked, and I impatiently wait for them to cool enough to eat. These are the longest minutes of the day. Despite blowing on the first heaping spoonful, I still manage to burn my mouth with the first bite. But it tastes so good I am not deterred.

Slowly I work away at the two pounds of pasta before me, a process that takes half an hour. I scrape the last remnants with my plastic spoon, wishing I could fit my head in the pot to lick the last bits, which still have a thin layer of warm yellow sauce on it. I slosh some water into it and grab some nearby leaves to scrape out the dregs. Then, I get up and scatter the thin soup into the rain far from my tarp.

By eight o'clock I'm digesting both my supper and

Dostoyevsky, the latter being the more difficult. Nonetheless I'm already so hooked into the story that I glance up with surprise from my small circle of light to find myself still in a wet autumn forest. But as the hours and pages pass, I call it a night.

Before going to sleep I put everything away in various plastic bags and stage my breakfast at the top of one of my food bags. For convenience, I have all my breakfast and lunch supplies in one bag, and my suppers and stove in another. I venture out one last time to hang them from a tree, to deter any bears and other critters from paying me a nighttime visit. I hope the miserable weather will also keep them away.

Back under the tarp, I strip off my down jacket, rain jacket, and rain pants to use as a pillow. With my headlamp off, I zip up my down bag in near-total darkness. As I lie back my eyes quickly adjust to the night, slowly revealing a night much lighter than I'd supposed. Perhaps the swollen moon above the clouds is light enough to diffuse its reflected rays. The fog has soaked up all sounds of the night but that of the gentle rain. I turn on my side and soon drift into sleep.

For most of the night I sleep on my stomach, and when I turn back onto my side I see that it is getting light. As I start the morning routine I look at my watch: three-fifty. I look up at the sky and see the moon is shining through a break in the clouds. The bright moonlight fooled me. Grateful for the extra time, I lay my head back down.

2

As the clouds brighten from slate to silver I open my eyes. The rain has stopped. Random rain drops, too swollen to hang on, drip down from the naked branches overhead. I pull my out down jacket and slide it on. I get dressed and fetch my stove, then get back into my sleeping bag while water boils for tea. The air is cool and still. I'm glad the rain has quit and hope it will stay away for a good while. I know of several good views down the trail today, and I would love to stop and enjoy them under clearer skies.

    I think back to the forecast I heard yesterday morning: the witch doctors of weather had predicted night winds and no rain. So, they were exactly wrong from my point of view.

When the water is ready I spoon some of the instant tea mix into the mug, along with a lump of powdered milk to give it some body. As I sip I start to pack up. First, I pull the bivy sack off my sleeping bag, noting that both are still fairly dry. The bivy sack goes into its own stuff sack, and I shove the sleeping bag into a garbage bag in the bottom of my backpack. I don't trust the raincover on my pack to keep the items inside dry, so everything but the food is double-bagged. Plus, I find that not using a stuff sack for the sleeping bag allows it to mold to whatever is placed on top of and around it, saving space.

I pull my rain pants over my long underwear and prepare to leave. Even though the night wasn't particularly cold, the hot tea really hits the spot. Because I am out of water, I forego breakfast and finish packing up the stove, sleeping pad, and tarp. By the time that's all squared away, I've finished my tea and put away the mug. I'm ready for Day 2.

By seven forty-five I'm striding back up to the trail where I left off yesterday afternoon. It's later than I hoped, but there's nowhere I have to be. Overcast days always make it harder to get going, even when I have a roof over my head. But as I hike along in the mist I feel my body warming up and contemplate hiking in just a t-shirt.

So far there is not much deadfall on the trail, just a log here and there. Despite the lack of expansive views there is plenty to see along the trail: in the naked brush spiders have constructed small, yet intricate cobwebs that show up well when wet. I pause several times to gaze at the miniature crystal palaces, and wonder how successful they are at catching prey. I try to take a photo with my camera, but it can't seem to find the proper focus, so I move on.

At a bend in the trail I find a suitable rivulet of water flowing over bare rock. The angle isn't ideal for my water bottle, so I pick up the biggest leaf I can find and curl it into a funnel. It works perfectly and soon my bottle is filled. I drop the iodine tabs in and keep moving. About half an hour later, when the water is suitably treated, I grab some mini-wheats and have a short breakfast.

Now the rain has started up again, and the tall brush along the trail sheds its water on me as I pass. With all the brush, this is not a good time to be on this section, but having no other options, I hike.

• • •

When I reach the spur trail up to White Rock, I take a bathroom break and pull out my camera for some pictures of the misty forest. If the day were clear, I would take the trail up and enjoy the panoramic views of the Boston Mountains, but there's little reason to do that now. A four-point buck saunters up the trail to within twenty feet of me. He is beautiful in the low, humid light. Being upwind, he is oblivious to my presence. He looks around curiously but unconcernedly and moves on. I wish him luck to get through hunting season. Then I turn back to the trail and head east and down.

There is a huge old oak down across the trail just past the junction. It is the first of many. The red oak borer hit hard here. It takes me an hour and a half to make my way down, around, and over all the trees in the two miles to Salt Fork Creek. Lucas was right: this section would be a nightmare going up. With the poor visibility, trying to see and find the trail markers is rather difficult, so I have to grid back and forth at times to find the trail.

Despite the hardship, my respect for the trail and trail maintainers is not diminished. I marvel that this small path through the woods is, in fact, a National Recreation Trail designated by Congress. What a wonderful thing.

Before long I start wondering if I'll see any hikers. Because I tend to hike in remote places wherever I go, I'm always curious to meet other people who seek out such places.

When I stop for a drink I see another deer. The doe approaches slowly until I take a step, then bounds off the ridge and down into the mist, flying the white flag of her tail. So far I've seen more deer than hikers. I like those odds. But with hunters out, I wonder how many more deer I'll see.

To keep my hiking progress steady, I decide to only take breaks at the mile markers. That will give me something to look forward to every twenty to thirty minutes, unless the clouds clear and allow views of the area.

By the time I reach Salt Fork Creek, the rain has petered out, but my pants and boots are soaking wet from all the brush along the trail. I cross the creek on rock, then stop for a rest and some water. So far I like the one water bottle approach. With streams common along the trail I'm never very far from water.

Soon I'm back at it, climbing up the west side of Potato Knob Mountain. There is less deadfall here, making the going that much easier. However, the brush here is high, wet, and thick, ensuring that I'll stay wet even without the rain.

The trail, too, is slick, so again I take my time on the rocky, leafy sections. I'm too clumsy too avoid a fall, so I prepare myself the best I can. It's only a matter of time before I do fall.

At the top, I cross a quiet forest road. Most of the mountains and ridges here have forest roads on them, though this one doesn't show any recent signs of traffic. Looking up, it appears that the clouds are thinning, though I see no blue sky. I'm excited for the next few miles, as it is one of the most beautiful places on the trail.

Here the trail follows on old road, closed to all but foot traffic. As I descend the wide path, I recall the last time I was here. The friends I was with told me they had adopted this section to maintain, and I can see today that they have done their job well. The condition is the best so far, and even appears to have been raked. Green grass is growing on the trail, even in now in November. I start singing, getting more and more excited to be near Spirit Creek. When I come within hearing distance of the stream, I see a patch of blue off to the southeast. It's almost lunchtime, and I'll be at the creek soon.

At the bottom, the trail runs parallel to the creek. Here I remember my dad and our friend Joel during their thru-hike two and a half years before. It is an idyllic spot spend time: the limestone cliff on the opposite side rises high above the milky green waters of Spirit Creek. Just upstream the water flows through a small, beautiful canyon. The trail ahead runs alongside it.

At the crossing I manage to rock-hop without getting too wet. Once on solid ground again I doff my pack and sit down for a long lunch. First, I pull out the filter to get some water. Using this I don't have to wait for the iodine to take effect. Instead I can tank up on as much as I want. A flash of blue reflecting in the water causes me to look up and see two large patches of blue sky. Surely, I think, the sun can break through. But a thick wall of low clouds obscures them by time I finish pumping water. Disappointed, I pull out my tortillas and cheese for lunch. I imagine lazing in the warm sun, listening to the soft whisper of the water.

I can't explain why, but there is a positive energy here. I find myself smiling unconsciously, feeling grateful that I'm here way out here in the woods next to this lovely creek. A woodpecker hammers away in the distance. This is exactly how I pictured the trip would be.

It is some time after I finish eating that I start getting ready to move again. I top up my water bottle again with good Spirit Creek water, then head up the trail. The views down into the rock-strewn creek are a good excuse to stop and enjoy the scenery. This would be a good area to set up a base camp and explore for a few days, especially in early spring when the temperatures are pleasant, but before the leaves are fully on.

As the trail leaves the creek it begins a short but steep climb up to Ragtown Road. In this area there are several medium-sized hillocks, possibly caused by the uneven settling of the limestone into sinkholes. Between the limestone and sandstone in these mountains, I bet there are an untold amount of caves. But being claustrophobic, I have no desire to explore them.

Up above the sun is still struggling to shine through the clouds. Ahead, a patch of light floats through the trees towards me and I stop and lift my face into the sunlight. The warmth feels wonderful. I suddenly feel giddy with delight, and thankful that the weather is improving. The light turns the trees into a rich golden hue.

Near the top of the climb, I gaze back to the west and see the two Potato Knobs between which the trail passed, distinct against the clearing sky. I also notice that a number of trees in this area still have their leaves, unlike the barren trees where I started. There are even a few green stragglers left as the last sign on life in these autumn woods. At least for plant life. No matter where I walk I still hear the twitters and chirps of the last brave birds here, scattering when I pass by.

An old weather-beaten trail register marks the end of the climb. I stop and fill out a card, hearing a vehicle pass by on Ragtown Road, but I'm unable to see it. It sounds awful, like an old hearse with the muffler gone and no shocks. When I cross the road shortly after, the smell of exhaust still hangs in the air.

It's time to start thinking about where to camp tonight. I pull out the guide as I walk, seeing that the terrain ahead will be either flat or downhill. I see Fane Creek is several miles ahead, and if memory serves correctly, there's a nice site beside it to camp. After a leisurely descent into a small hollow, the easiest section of the trail begins.

A hundred or so years ago, a spur line from a nearby railroad ran through here to carry the prized and profitable white oaks that grew on these hillsides. Though the tracks are gone, the bed of the spur line serves as the trail for the next three miles. Except for a few downed trees that require climbing over, it is pleasant walking. I track my pace with my watch and the mile markers, averaging just over three miles an hour—my best pace so far.

As I come to a cut through the side of a hill, I see a whitetail buck on the left that hasn't yet detected me. I stop and watch as noses the ground. He is much bigger than the buck I saw back near White Rock, and I start to count the points on his rack. In silhouette it is difficult to make out which is his rack and which are branches, but I can definitely make out six. But just then he finally sees me and skedaddles down the hill.

Off to my left I can see the sunshine lighting up the forest across the valley. The sky is now almost completely clear and blue. That and the easy walking make the distance pass by dreamily.

Soon I come to a double blaze, which marks where the trail leaves the old railbed and starts descending down to

Fane. My left knee begins to ache as I head down, but I don't mind so much now that the sun is shining and camp is not far away.

A ways further, a clearing appears off to my left, so I check my guidebook. It says it's a wildlife food plot, I suppose for hard times. There is also a small pond here that had been bulldozed up in case of drought. I imagine that it'd be a good place to stalk deer, if I were so inclined.

I don't hunt and never have, not out of any moral or ideological objections, but simply because I am too lazy. I don't have any hard feelings towards the hunters, as most of them are out here to put food on the table. They're hunters, as opposed to sportsman or trophy hunters—they're the ones I have a problem with. Both kinds argue that they are needed to control the deer population, which only makes sense because we eliminated any potential predators years ago. Now that we've started managing them, we have to keep on doing it in a bureaucratic cycle. We need nature and it needs us. But I really wonder if all these wildlife plots and ponds are really necessary or are just here for the benefit of the hunters. I think I know what the answer is, too.

But I'm not out here to worry about politics, government, or anything else besides how far to hike, where to sleep, what to eat, how my body will handle the hiking, and where to take a shit. Those are my only pressing needs out here.

At the bottom of the hill the trail takes a right to follow Fane Creek downstream. There is a lovely stand of pines here, so I start looking for a place to camp. Pines are my preferred place to camp, as the thick carpet of needles under them makes for a soft bed.

Where the trail turns to cross the creek there is a splendid campsite, complete with a large fire ring and several built-up stone seats circling it. A few feet away are several flat open sites under the pines for me to pitch the tarp. And after the tarp is up, I go down to the creek and filter water for the evening. The slab of rock that spans the creek here is marvelous.

Now comes my favorite time of day: teatime. As I get the water to heating, I eat a couple of fig newtons and a protein bar. The food and tea make me feel warm and relaxed as I look up at the afternoon sky. It looks like it will be a clear night, though it still feels damp here.

I while away the last of the afternoon reading and

taking an occasional stroll over to the creek for quiet contemplation. As evening falls I doze off over my book, but am awakened by a truck passing on a dirt road about a hundred yards away. After only a few seconds the noise is gone.

    A chill has descended on the camp, so I put on my thermal top and jacket, as well as my fleece-lined wool beanie. Normally I'd have opted for a lighter option, but I believe in taking one luxury item on every backpacking trip and this one is it. It's been with me on my memorable trips to Nepal, Tanzania, and South America, so I feel it is appropriate out here, too.

    After the early sunset I dig my headlamp out of the top pouch of my backpack so I can continue reading. From my bed under the tarp I watch the moon rise over the flanks of Whiting Mountain to the east. The light is nearly bright enough to read by, but a large cloud soon drifts over, leaving me in the dark.

    The sixteen-plus miles I hiked today have greatly amplified my hunger. I can barely wait till seven to cook my supper. On the side of the fire pit there is a perfect slab on which to put my stove. As the noodles boil, bright rays of white moonlight break through the clouds and filter down into the grove of pines. The whole area is lit with a ghostly silver light, so I turn off my headlamp and finish cooking without it.

The stone benches are still wet from the rain, so I flip one over and sit on it as I eat in the moonlight. The moon has given the night a sort of magical feel, perhaps because it is full. A few stars shine through the dense canopy. I can see no other lights, nor hear anything else besides the waters of Fane Creek whispering nearby. Alone in the forest. Looking around camp, I see the moon shining down on my tarp through a break in the trees, making it appear to glow in the surrounding darkness.

With a belly full of two pounds of noodles, I clean out my cooking pot and put away the food before retiring to the tarp for more reading. Sixty pages in and it seems like the story has yet to really begin. I wonder if I should've brought something else more direct, like a Jim Harrison or Cormac McCarthy book. Or hell, some Jung to crack open the subconscious with all the quiet time to think. But I can't change it now, so Fyodor D. it is.

The fatigue quickly builds as I read, and finally overcomes me. With the moon high overhead, I call it a night and crawl into my bag and bivy. I think of my girlfriend, two thousand miles away, and then think back over the day. I linger over thoughts of Spirit Creek before sleep overtakes me, and am soon dreaming.

3

Mist hangs thickly in the morning sky as dew drips lightly from the pines. Here in the creek bottom the air is quite cold, prodding me to pack up quickly as soon as I emerge from the cocoon of my sleeping bag. Unlike yesterday, I eat a full breakfast of cereal before setting out on the trail.

The single biggest climb of the whole hike looms before me: a 1500-foot climb up and over Whiting Mountain. The only time I've hiked it I was carrying a daypack with one water bottle, as opposed to the load I have now.

But before I can start the climb I have to wade across Fane Creek, which is a frigid prospect this cold morning.

Perhaps out of reluctance, I don't get underway until after eight—a very late start considering that it's been light for more than an hour. With my sandals on I ford the shallow, icy water over the smooth slab of rock I'd admired yesterday evening. On the other side I emerge with numb red feet, which I quickly dry and put back into socks and boots. Shouldn't take long to get them warmed up again.

    Back into the hike, I cross a dirt road and start heading up the hill. The sun is shining brightly through the fog now, and I imagine how nice the day will be once the fog lifts. The birds seem to be celebrating already, with their energetic activity both in the trees and on the trail ahead of me.

    The grade of trail here makes for pleasant walking. It alternately climbs and levels off, as opposed to one long pull. With a pack full of water, including the two-liter bottle, the gentle terrain helps me keep a steady pace.

    Looking at the guidebook last night I saw that the next reliable water source was sixteen miles away, hence the extra load of water. I'm relatively certain I'll pass more flowing water between here and there, but in the end, didn't want to take the chance of being high and dry. I know from experience how much a case of even mild dehydration can ruin a beautiful hike.

During a quick snack break the sun finally breaks through and lights up the forest. Dew-covered cobwebs stand in crystal relief among the wet brushy branches. It's going to be a good day.

Out of the creek bottom the air is warm and spring-like. Since the elevation gain is spread over four miles I'm able to keep a two-mile an hour pace, and credit it to the welcome feeling of sunshine on my skin. Despite the backpack, I feel light on my feet and strong and in my legs.

The only trouble I run into is a regeneration area, an area the Forest Service has turned into a brushy, overgrown jungle on the nose of a ridge. Between the brush and the deadfall I lose the trail. At least the bush here is mostly dry, so my pants and boots don't get soaked. I grid back and forth over more downed trees before I see a blaze and walk towards it.

The view to the south, through an opening in the trees, is quite pretty here. I can easily see the Mulberry River Valley, the most prominent nearby drainage, and a wonderful floating stream when the water's up. The trail crosses the upper part of the Mulberry many miles and several days ahead.

From here I can also see that I still have a good deal of uphill to go. For now, though, the trail runs flat on an arm of the mountain, with decent views off both sides. As I begin the last grunt to the top I focus on the fig newtons that will be my reward when I get there, so I resolve not to stop till then. This is the only strenuous part of the climb, but it doesn't last long. Soon enough the top is in view and I cross a road on top. Nearby there is a deer camp in a small clearing, but it looks vacant. With my hungry stomach, I wonder if any of these hunters would offer me food. A beer would be welcome, too.

I follow the road to where the trail dives off the east side of the ridge, and soon find a familiar flat place in the trail to sit for snack time. The trees have definitely grown up since I was last here, a number of years ago. I believe this may have even been one of my first day hikes on the trail.

The view to the east encompasses much of the terrain through which I'll soon be hiking. I can even make out what I think is Hare Mountain, where I intend to have lunch. As I sit I can tell my legs want to move, but my stomach wants to stay and eat more. So, I take a slug of water and put my pack back on. According to my watch it's been almost exactly two hours since I left camp, a distance of four miles. I hope to make twelve more before stopping for the day, at least six hours away. With the fine weather and good spirits that shouldn't be too difficult.

Below and out of sight of the trail runs a state highway. I can hear the semi trucks gearing down for the descent into the little town I see down in the bottomland. They are noisy, but gone soon enough.

After the trail hits a level, rocky bench, it comes to a mudslide. Only about twenty feet has been washed away, likely from a spring storm that caused numerous floods all over the state. According to the news then, rivers were hitting levels that hadn't been seen in years, if ever. I'd heard there would be mudslides on the trail, some of them significant. I carefully negotiate this one and continue onwards.

As the trail winds along a small bluff I keep an eye out for a rock house, built by early settlers in the day. Fortunately, the trail runs right up to it, so I stop and take a look inside. The mortared stone walls are still holding strong, and the two doorways are sighted for especially good views of the highland scenery. I can't help but admire the craftsmanship and esthetic sense of the builder.

In the back I check a stone basin for water, but it appears the spring has dried up, or found a new outlet. I'm not worried about water yet, as I've still got the full two-liter bottle in my pack. I take a second out front to refill the small water bottle and drink it all before moving on.

With the highway coming into view just below, I see a trail register just ahead. I stop and check the entries to see if there are any other hikers out and about. The most recent entry is from Lucas, several days before. I don't see any cars in the small parking lot below the road, either.

As I cross the highway, I imagine it'll be the last paved road I'll walk on for days. Good. Another semi passes after I disappear into the woods, making me more glad to be away from the roads. But surely, I think, I will see some hikers in the next day or two. The twenty-mile section I'm beginning is one of the most scenic and popular on the trail, and with the nice weather I'm willing to bet there is at least one other brave hiker out here in the woods with me.

Not far below the highway I find a small stream, and decide to refill my bottle, in case it's the last stream for a while. With the temperature warming, I'll be going through water faster than on the past two cloudy days. And by the time I reach Fly Gap several miles later, I've nearly finished the bottle off again. Checking the guide, I see that there's a potential water source about a mile ahead, so I hold off dipping further into my reserve.

Sure enough, just after I reach another roadbed I come to a narrow ravine that has an ample flow of water—surprising this close to the top of the ridge. I think all my worries about water a bit foolish, and wonder whether I needed to hike with extra two liters at all. But water is the most precious resource to be had out here, and I'd rather have too much than too little.

Ahead to the east I can see a good-sized hill: Hare Mountain, the highest point on the trail. It takes me a while, but soon, after a short climb up from the ravine, I reach the top, elevation 2380 feet. Because the lowest point in these immediate parts is about 600 feet, the view from here is amazing. Off to the south, I can see the highest point in the state: Mount Magazine, a broad, free-standing, and flat-topped mass at an elevation of 2753 feet.

The Ozark Mountains are not typical mountains like the Rockies or Smokys. They were formed by the uplift of the Ozark Plateau, and subsequent erosion carved the creeks and river valleys that I hike through today. As a result, the moutaintops here are usually flat. So, instead of being rewarded with a craggy summit, one is rewarded with a flat walk alongside or through a meadow when reaching a mountaintop.

Taking advantage of the flat ground, many early farms sprung up on these mountaintops, including at Hare Mountain. Here, an enterprising settler cleared the trees and rocks, using the latter to build a picturesque stone wall along which the trail runs. Despite an age of a hundred years or more, it is mostly intact.

I take off my pack here and find the perfect viewpoint to take a longer look at the scenery. Besides Mount Magazine, I see the Mulberry River valley and its tributaries just to the south, along with a number of rolling, wooded ridges. A warm, pleasant breeze is blowing here, so I find a flat limestone slab on which to have lunch. But before eating, I take out my dew-soaked tarp and hang it between two nearby trees to dry in the sun. Sitting in the sunshine with my lunch at hand, I relish my good fortune to be here on such a magnificent day.

After my peanut butter tortilla I eat a large handful of my trail mix. Mentally I start making preparations to leave, and the body soon follows. I take some ibuprofen for my knee and slowly pack up my things. My tarp feels wonderfully crisp and dry as I stow it away. With everything buttoned up, I take a few long seconds to savor the view one last time, and begin the next descent.

The views off the side of this ridge are lovely, and I take it slow so I can enjoy them. I try to pick out where the trail will go next, but am not sure. Soon I'm back in the timber, where the light wind is rustling the leaves, stirring up the earthy smell I associate with fall. My mood, boosted by lunch and ibuprofen, is great. Besides my girlfriend, there's nothing else I'm missing right now.

As I hike I figure I'll reach the next major creek, Herrod's, around four. Checking the guide I note there is a short climb just after Herrod's, leading to a saddle off of Herrian Mountain, where I might get a good view of the sunset. Perhaps even the sunrise. I tentatively plan to camp there, which would have the additional benefit of staying above the cold sink in the creek bottom. Because Herrod's Creek is fairly sizeable drainage, it would most certainly hold a good bit of cold air through the night. A ridge, on the other hand, would be both drier and warmer. I put off the definite decision until I reach Herrod's and see how tired I am, but the idea is getting more appealing.

A narrow, rocky ravine marks the end of the descent. In the springtime, or after a big rain, there are a number of waterfalls in this area. Unfortunately for me they are dry today, though the boulders and cliffs here are beautiful in their own right, the kind of scenery that is the essence of the Ozarks.

Sure enough, it is about four o'clock when I reach Herrod's Creek, which I'm able to cross dry. There are several possible campsites here, both of which I've used before. But it was also here that Lucas told me a bear had approached his camp several days ago, surprising the hell out of him. I can only imagine his startled Cajun face. Luckily for him the bear wasn't aggressive, but I don't want to test my luck here tonight and see if it comes back.

My mind made up, I start on up to the saddle. I'm down in the shadows, where the chill is already settling in, but not far above I see the sunset line. Thinking I can catch it and make it to a good viewpoint before sundown, I take an Emergen-C for energy and make my way swiftly up the trail, regaining the daylight.

Just off to the right of the trail there is a small creek, still running with water. I need to top off before camp, but wanting to see the sunset, I keep going. But as the trail swings away from the creek, I groan to discover that there is no more water flowing—it had dried up back down the trail. I take a quick inventory, realizing that I have enough for supper, but not much more. Perhaps there'll be something further up.

As I reach a pine grove I can see that I'm near the top. There is a bit of flat ground here, but not much. At the saddle there is a two track that runs right beside a wildlife pond. I don't particularly like filtering out of standing water, but if I want water for the morning I have no choice. I chide myself for not filling up earlier, but I'd been too focused on getting up here to think of much else.

For my labors, I get to see the sun set over Hare Mountain. It is spectacular, a gorgeous, glorious final fireball to end the hiking day. For those moments my thoughts dissipate and mind becomes clear and calm. The forest around me is silent. It was worth the rush and worry to witness such beauty.

As the last rays of the dying sun stain the clouds pink, I keep hiking, looking for a place to sleep. After I cross the two-track, I hear the whine of a truck approaching from the north. As it comes into view it slows down, possibly seeing the orange vest on my pack. I keep moving on and so do they.

Suddenly it occurs to me that I'm making the same mistake again: rushing onwards when I could stay put. I backtrack to the road and find a spot under the pines where I can set up camp. Before putting up the tarp, I recon the pond to see if the water is worth filtering. I make sure to take the orange vest off my pack and put it on, in case the hunters come back.

Even in the failing light I can tell the pond is murky. I failed to bring a bandanna or similar item to put over my filter to screen out the extra sediment, but it's too late to stop now. As I pump I can feel the resistance growing—the filter is clogging. Luckily I'm able to fill both water bottles before it gets stuck.

In the last of twilight I set up the tarp and arrange my bedding under it. I see a jeep approaching, a different one than before and heading the opposite direction. It slows as it comes into view, undoubtedly drawn by the vest and hurried motions of my camp-making. But it keeps going without stopping.

As soon as everything is set up and I stop moving, I feel the evening chill come on. I put on my jacket and eat a snack as I boil water. Watching night fall, I really feel the fatigue setting in. I've hiked nearly eighteen miles today.

The tea revives me, removing the fog from my brain, so I get my book and headlamp to find out what the Karamazov Brothers are up to. At last the story is getting really interesting with the beginnings of intrigue. Now I'm not minding the extra weight so much.

For supper tonight are two packets of teriyaki rice. For some reason I have been infatuated with rice all my life, making it hard for me to go a few days without it. And after two nights of pasta and eighteen miles of trail, I'm craving it. It proves trickier to cook, and the smell only sharpens my savage appetite. I check out the information on the label, seeing that the total for both meals will be 1300 calories. The more the better, as I'm burning double what I would be sitting around the house.

After savoring each and every salty-sweet bite, I lay back, careful not to disturb my full belly. Though tempted to go to sleep then, I wash the pot and get my things arranged for the night. With my food packed away I hang my food bags in a pine tree, hoping Lucas' bear stays away tonight.

As I walk back to my site, I notice the chill in the air is gone. Perhaps the cold air has already sunk down into the drainage. It feels pleasant enough for me to unzip my jacket and take off my beanie. My decision to camp up here seems smarter all the time, I tell myself smugly.

An owl hooting from a nearby tree startles me as I sit down. It has to be very close. I turn off my headlamp and listen in the dark, unable to pinpoint where it is calling from. As it hoots again, I can feel chills go up my spine. After a long pause I hear another hoot from farther away. I wish I could see it, as I think owls are perhaps the most beautiful birds. Quiet, too: I don't hear it fly away.

After moonrise the coyotes come out. I've seldom heard them out here, and have never seen them. Tonight it sounds like there are a lot of them. One is very close: I can hear the leaves rustling underneath its paws, when it's not yelping. A few dogs join in the chorus from down in the valley. Perhaps the moon has got them all riled up.

    I feel quite the opposite: with the bright moon shining down on my tarp I lay back to watch the night, but am soon dreaming.

4

After a night of vivid dreams of food and my girlfriend, the dawn comes slow and bleary. The overcast sky to matches my mood. I arise sluggishly, a dull ache thudding in my head. The majestic sunrise I'd hoped for is nowhere to be seen.

Thinking I might have a touch of dehydration, I take a long pull of water and pour a large batch of water for tea. I vaguely recall that the meal last night had something like 150% of the RDA for sodium, which probably didn't help.

The morning mountain air is cool, but not cold. I didn't even fully zip up my sleeping bag during the night. Also, the tarp and bivy sack are dry, making them much easier to pack away. No evidence of hunters this morning.

As I load up my pack, I finish the last of my breakfast. The liquids and food make me feel better already. Checking the guide, I make a tentative plan to make it a short day, hoping to make it to the Little Mulberry River Valley. I recall a nice campsite in the area that has both good views and water nearby.

Without the sun to gauge the time, I'm surprised to see that I'm on the trail right at seven o'clock. Several miles ahead there is a wonderful scenic area in which I'd like to take my time, so I hike steadily to get there. But before I get there I find myself truly enjoying the descent into Indian Creeek. I feel light, and the walking is easy. Around me, the woods are quiet and beautiful.

Near the 50-mile mark, I enter a gorgeous stand of birches. Even the little trees have at least a few rust-colored leaves still hanging from their gray branches. Some of the older trees are so large that I cannot reach my arms around them.

A memory from my childhood comes vividly to me. We are visiting my grandparents, and I try to reach my arms around my grandfather, but cannot. He was a large man, and it was years before I could. When that day came I felt like a big man myself. My grandfather surely laughed at me, the youngest and smallest of his grandchildren. And though these trees are indeed beautiful, they are nowhere near as colorful as he was. He would surely be chuckling if he could see me now.

    A child of the Great Depression, he was a thoroughly practically and jolly man. When my Dad and I took up backpacking in my high school years, he viewed it with disdain and disbelief. Perhaps it was his time in the Army that made tramping through the hills seem so useless.

    "Why would you want to carry forty-five pounds up and down hills for *fun?*" he would ask us, shaking his head. I could never give a decent answer then, and even now it is difficult for me to articulate.

    But as I walk along the moss-covered trail beside the smooth-bark beeches, I come as close as I can to voicing it. The simplicity: the sound of a stream flowing through limestone boulders. The sunsets and sunrises. Watching vultures circle in the thermals beside stark, broken cliffs. The color of moonlight shining through the nighttime forest.

Walking on a path so seldom trodden that a bright green carpet of moss grows underfoot.

Every step this morning brings a new reason to be here. I only wish my grandfather were here, so I could tell him.

Even down here in the drainage, I can hear the wind whipping over the ridgetops. Though warm and pleasant for now, it seems like the cold front predicted for the next few days is blowing in. The clouds still appear to be high, not the low ones that typically bring rain.

To cross Indian Creek I go barefoot. The cold water takes my breath away, but the stones in the stream feel wonderful on my feet. When I have my socks and boots back on, I begin the climb up and over to Briar Branch. As I gain elevation I can feel the wind at my back, increasing the higher I go. As I enter a large stand of pines, I notice the tops are swaying in large ovals. But in the wind, I still trust them more than the hardwoods. Some of the hardwoods have rot in the middle, making them more likely to drop branches in these conditions. It would not be a good time to be back near White Rock, with all the dead red oaks waiting to fall.

Winding through the pines, the trail comes alongside a

bluff, with a steep drop into the drainage below. This is Briar Branch, and the views are great both up and down drainage. Across the valley I see a notch in the opposite ridge: I bet that is where the trail is headed. As I head down the hill, I leave the sweet smell of pine behind me.

Long before I can see it, I can hear the gentle rush of creekwater over stone. Much like Spirit Creek two days before, slate-colored sandstone bluffs rise over Briar Branch. I pass a perfect campsite just before crossing the creek, noting it as a possibility for future hikes. Here again the beeches crowd above and below the bluffs, enriching the scenery even in the half-light of this overcast day. With all the bluffs in this area, there must be dozens of waterfalls when the water's up. The soft whisper of the wind in the trees sings in harmony with the song of the creek. I'm in the Marinoni now.

The Marinoni Scenic Area was named for a friend of the founder of the trail, Tim Ernst. I pass the wooden sign explaining the name and honoring Mr. Marinoni, admiring the uniquely-shaped stump from which it was made. There is flat ground nearby, so I take a break.

The drainage here, the upper part of Briar Branch, is quite narrow and sheltered. As a result the air is more humid, and I see small ferns and other plants emerge from nearly every break in the bluff wall here. Also, the rocks wear a thick coat of slick moss—treacherous to walk on, but still beautiful. I feel that I can sit in this spot for hours and still not take it in. In a word, this is peaceful.

The groggy feeling I had when I awoke this morning is now long gone. As I put my pack back on, I can tell it's getting lighter. And so am I: I have to tighten the waist strap a bit more almost to the end.

Heading upstream, I try to make my way up and over a downed beech. It, and all the rocks around it, are all slick. I find myself slipping at every step, falling several times. But the only damage is to my pride, and a few muddy streaks on my pants.

After crossing the creek a few more times I leave the Marinoni behind and head up and out of Briar Branch. On top of the ridge I cross the usual dirt road, and begin another gentle descent. Up above, the sun is peeking through the clouds, warming the air.

In the distance I can already see the Little Mulberry River Valley. Also in the distance is someone shooting targets—sounds like a .22 pistol. The shots come quick and high from off to the right. As the trail winds down into the next drainage I know I'm getting closer, and don't really want to be. I have nothing against guns, I just don't want to be hit by any stray bullets—a genuine concern considering the volume of fire. I hardly notice the bluff I'm walking on.

As I make it to the drainage bottom, the shooting abruptly stops. Good. There is a trailhead just down the way that next to a nice creek, and since I'm low on water I'd like to take a quiet break there. Soon I see the trailhead register and as usual, I check the cards for any recent activity. The only recent entry is from Lucas. I do enjoy the fact that he filled out cards both outbound and inbound.

Just across the forest road is a good place to get water, so I dig out my filter and some fig newtons for a snack. A white Geo Tracker passes as I'm pumping water, but either does not see or does not acknowledge my wave. I doubt they've seen many hikers around here, much less right by the creek.

After the filtering, I sprawl out on the ground and consult my guide. The spot I hope to camp at tonight is only about four miles away, and it's only ten o'clock. So I figure on getting there sometime in the noon hour, barring any unforeseen events. I pack up the filter, take another pull of water, and head back into the woods. The cease-fire is still in effect.

The clouds have cleared enough to let the sun through in pieces. Even though the temperature is only in the 60s, it's starting to feel rather muggy. I debate taking off my shirt to keep it from soaking through, but figure it would be better to keep it on to avoid pack chafe. And soon enough the clouds close, shutting out the sun. No tanning today. I can also hear the wind picking up, and wonder if a storm is making up. Ahead, the next ridge is looming bigger and bigger.

A narrow strip of woods, running beside a nearly-straight stream, marks an easement through a farmer's field. Green bottomland grass grows on both sides. For some reason I like this short section very much. At the end I can see the beginning of a road walk.

Despite following a number of old, decommissioned roads through the Ozarks, there is actually very little road-walking on the trail. All I can think of is this section, a few miles up by the Buffalo River, and the road crossings. That's it. Just a small fraction of the entire length of the trial.

I have this section all to myself. I cross the concrete

bridge over the Little Mulberry, and then begin the next long climb. The valley here is wide and picturesque: farm buildings are scattered widely. Not much traffic passes this way.

Where the trail leaves the road, the square metal hiker sign has been shot up so much that there are only a few spots of paint left on it. The rest is bare, perforated metal. It seems that most forest signs double as targets.

After a decent climb I stop and take an Emergen-C. I can feel the air starting to cool, and the wind shows no sign of stopping. I still have about a thousand feet of elevation gain over the next two miles. I hope there will be water where I remember it. There's always something to worry about out here.

In a few minutes I feel a wonderful burst of energy, and increase my pace up the climbs and surge ahead on the flats. Even though I ate less than an hour ago, my stomach is already calling for more. The urge to get to camp and eat again keeps me on pace, though I occasionally slow to enjoy the views of the river valley below. I don't tarry long, as the wind chills the sweat on my back.

Up ahead I see the trail heading towards a ravine, which I believe is close to my intended camp. The welcome sound of rushing water greets me as I come around the bend, passing mile marker 60. I try to take a picture of the small waterfall there, but can't get the right angle without having to hang onto a nearby tree. As I turn, I slip backwards and grab the tree for dear life. My camera dangles from the wrist strap as I carefully bring my feet back up to solid ground and step away.

After I cross the stream I can see where I want to camp. And a few strides later I'm there. I look at my watch: twelve fifteen. Time to eat, relax, and enjoy the afternoon. But first, I take off my boots and put on my sandals. The cushion on the balls of my feet are nearly gone, and they are smarting. The sandals help a bit, but not nearly as much as I'd hoped. I grab my lunch bag and shuffle over to the bluff: there's a flat pedestal of rock with a great view that looks like the perfect lunch spot.

The wind has turned cold now, and is blowing hard on the more exposed west side of the ridge. I sit beside a rock, hoping it will shield me from the wind, and practically inhale my tortillas. A shiver prompts me to leave my perch and grab another layer from my pack.

I decide to start camp chores, this time starting with

water. Having the creek nearby is handy, and I get the filter, and both bottles to take over there with me. Through the trees I see movement on the trail: a dog? Another hiker? Then I see the flourish of white and the doe bounds back down the trail.

A small ledge beside the creek makes a convenient spot to pump, and I laboriously fill my bottles. The pump feels clogged from the pond, but at least the pumping warms me. I figure I'll try to rinse the inner filter after I have tea.

As I return to camp, I notice the clouds in the distance are darker and lower. Rain is on the way. I pick out a nice flat spot for my tarp and quickly get it set up, despite the gusty winds. I stash my pack under it, then set up the stove to get the water going. As it heats, I watch the clouds track more to the north than at me. I hope the rain will pass, but the clouds stretch as far as I can see.

Instead of hunkering under the tarp, I take my foam pad and find a nice tree under which to sit and drink my tea and read. Now *this* feels like camping: sitting under an oak with a hot drink and a good book. Despite the ominous sky I feel relaxed and happy.

The trees are blocking much of the wind, and I feel only the occasional cold gust. But overhead the trees are swaying.

As I get comfortable, I notice a dark splotch on a page of my book. Sure enough, rain. I gather up the sleeping bag, book, and tea mug and take shelter underneath the tarp.

Dostoyevsky will be the entertainment this afternoon. It'll be a long afternoon of reading, but at least I can catch up. Only 700 pages or so to go. If the first part is any indication, there will be plenty of treachery, drunkenness, stabbing, and backstabbing to keep me occupied. I no longer regret the choice or the weight of it.

As the rain picks up, the wind dies down. It is getting colder, and before long I can I see my exhalations. I take off my boots and pull out my sleeping bag. It's only two o'clock, but I feel that I need it. I pitched the tarp so that the low end is pointing directly into the wind, and it's doing a good job of keeping the rain out.

By four the rain has dwindled to an occasional patter. A few breaks of blue appear overhead, making me think there might be a dramatic sunset in store. I retrieve the stove and food bags from the fire ring back to the tarp. At the high end, there is plenty of room to sit and cook, and stay dry in the process. I'm looking forward to a hot drink to wake up me up. Two hours of laying around and reading has left me drowsy.

While the water is heating, I drift into a hungry daydream about all things hot and greasy to eat. Along with ice cream, milkshakes, root beer, beer, etc. I look down at the chalky filling of my protein bar and sigh, knowing that in half an hour I'll be just as hungry as before. But the tea tastes great and I take advantage of the break in the rain to walk around and stretch my legs.

During the last two days I feel that I'm hitting my stride. The hiking is going smoothly and I'm recovering well from each day's effort. Camp chores are automatic and getting more efficient each day. Despite the bit of trouble from my left IT band, my legs have been feeling good—not even sore. The only problem I'm having is the balls of my feet. They're taking a real beating, something I hadn't anticipated. They've hurt more and earlier each day. I hope all this rest this afternoon will help them, and they'll toughen up for the coming days.

Looking off to the west I see another huge swath of dark clouds, darker than before. No sunset views tonight. As cold as it is, I wonder if this next round will bring snow, an appealing prospect. It's not nearly as dreary as rain, and is my easier to sweep off clothing, the tarp, etc. Plus it provides more traction in mud, if it's not covering up the ice. And best of all, it turns the woods into a winter wonderland. I do believe that is my favorite time to be in the woods, when it's covered with snow and all is white and silent. It'll be interesting to see if that happens.

 After my walk I return to my bed and book. Once again I find myself engrossed in the story, caught up in the Karamazov Brothers' intrigue. Though my mind is occupied, my belly is not. After a few furious minutes of grumbling, I start supper.

As soon as the water starts boiling the rain starts up again, with an occasional spat of sleet. Tonight it's noodles with some generic creamy and buttery sauce. As my friend Pete was fond of saying: "Hunger is the best sauce." And I've got plenty of that tonight.

The rain peters out as I eat, and I notice the clouds beginning to break up. A few stars are visible through the bare branches above, and soon a light begins to brighten the eastern horizon. In a wonder of good timing, the clouds are all gone by the time the moon begins to rise through the trees, and I have a front row seat to watch it. With each sliver of moon that appears, my excitement grows. I couldn't have planned it better. I finish my supper in record time—just a shade under forty-five minutes—and make a quick job of washing the pot and tidying up. It's time to take a walk in the moonlight.

Stars dot the dome of the night sky overhead without a single blemish of cloud. I walk over to the bluffline, pointing my headlamp at any holes or cracks that might pitch me over and beyond. Down below I can see a few scattered lights twinkle up and down the Little Mulberry Valley. I imagine the folks down there warming themselves up beside their cast iron stoves or stacked-rock fireplaces.

Across the valley on the opposite ridge I see a few more lights, likely from hunters' camps. Part of me yearns for human contact, to talk with them and tell them about all I've seen.

Wistfully surveying the valley, I debate building a fire. There's not much wood to be found around here—a lot of it has already been used by previous campers. Plus, any wood I find has been soaking for much of the day. I gaze upward and decide that a down bag under a clear sky will suffice.

After a short jaunt up the trail, I return to camp for the final round of reading. I munch on some trail mix to stoke the internal fire, thinking back over my day. I'm glad I took it easy today. I feel reenergized and ready to get back at it tomorrow.

After some more of the book, I turn to the guide to plan for the morning. The first ten miles look relatively flat, then some downhill and more flat after that. All this rest has made me more ambitious: I feel like trying a twenty-mile day. With good weather and trail conditions, it is certainly possible.

My only concern is that the creek crossings will be high and dangerous. My previous trek in these parts was under such conditions: it was springtime and it had rained all night, over-saturating the ground and turning the creeks into muddy, swollen rivers. I recall the first ford being the deepest, up to my crotch. As I crossed I quartered downstream to lessen the resistance of the water, but it still nearly swept me off my feet. The subsequent crossings weren't as deep, but just as swift and slick. It was borderline dangerous, the most uneasy I'd ever felt fording a creek, and I've done a lot of them.

On the list of objective dangers out here, high water crossings are at the top. I learn from reading the guide that the only known fatality on the trail was at the crossing of the Upper Mulberry River, another day's hike away. I get chills when I read that today is the fourteenth anniversary of that death, a hiker from New York with the last name of Boomer. There is a creek ahead that is named after him. Not exactly a bright thought to take to sleep with me.

All afternoon and even now, the combination of the wind and the nearby creek sound like a large waterfall. It's a kind of music to me, filling the air. Or better yet, a kind of white noise to soak up all the other sounds into one soothing tune: the white noise of the woods.

By nine forty-five I'm nearly falling over with sleep, so I put the book away and arrange my pillow before turning off my headlamp. I lay on my right side, gazing at the stars shining far off to the north and trying not to think of creek crossings till tomorrow.

5

Well before my alarm goes off, my internal clock wakes me in the early morning darkness. The hood of sleeping bag is cinched around my face, so that only my nose is exposed. And while the rest of body is warm and dry, I can feel the cold stain of condensation on my moustache.

By the official wake-up time of six, I'm wide awake with martial music sounding in my head. The thought of a Big Day is pumping me up already, though the frost and frigid air give me pause before I unzip my bag and commit myself to the cold. And despite having bedded down under clear skies, a depressing layer of gray clouds once again hangs overhead.

A cold autumn breeze is blowing as I pack up the last of my gear. There is a fine layer of frozen rain on the tarp that I try to shake off, but my hands become so wet and numb that I simply cram it in the stuff sack, ice and all. The tiny guy lines that I tied to the anchor points prove particularly difficult to gather and wind with the limited movement in my bare fingers. I use my tea mug to warm up my pink hands after packing my gear, and am ready to go.

I take off down the trail at seven fifteen, striding quickly for warmth. The trail stays close to the bluffline for the next mile and a half, and I don't stop at all. The view and the light is much the same as it was yesterday afternoon, only the air is much colder. It's turning out to be very similar to the last time I hiked, and that is not a good thing.

Where the trail leaves the bluffline, I take out my camera and take a quick picture. The bitter wind brings tears to my eyes when I face it. The gray clouds don't show signs of rain, at least not yet. As I head into the woods the wind dies off, but not comfortable enough to shed layers. But the walking is easy and I am able to maintain a quick pace and make good time.

Along the way I pass a cabin, which looks both inviting

and vacant. No cars or other signs of life are present. I amble closer to have a look, and see that it appears to still be under construction: the door onto the upstairs deck is missing, as well as a good part of the porch. The remote location is perfect, far from any town or highway. The road into it doesn't look like it gets much use either. I admire it for a few more moments and move on.

Around nine o'clock I take my first break, feeling the hunger in my belly. A thick, downed oak beside the trail looks like a good place, so I take off my pack and sit down. For a snack I pull out the bag of cereal which, though I've been working on it for five days now, looks nearly full. The mini wheats are disintegrating from getting bumped around by other things in my food bag and pack, so I have to pour them into my mouth, rather than eat them by hand. But they taste good, giving me some much-needed sugar, and I chase them with a couple of fig newtons as a bonus.

I reckon I've gone about five miles so far this morning, and my energy is good. On a lark, I put on another pair of socks over the ones I'm wearing to help cushion the balls of my feet. Though they haven't been hurting yet, I want to prepare them for the pounding I plan to give them today.

Putting my feet back into the boots, they feel snug but not overly tight. I loosen the laces a bit to make them more comfortable.

Soon I'm off again, heartened to see a few breaks in the clouds. I suspect, though, the clouds will be around the rest of the day. The sky just has that kind of look to it. I'm hoping for a good sunset, like the one I got to see night before last.

With only the trees to look at and the cold driving me on, I keep grinding out the miles. I should have no problem getting in ten miles by twelve o'clock; in fact I might even have the ten miles by eleven, a new personal record.

Up ahead I hear a four-wheeler: I must be getting close to another road. Soon, I smell the sweet scent of woodsmoke. As I top out on a little rise, I find myself walking into a well-constructed and well-supplied hunters' camp. A steady cloud of smoke pours from the metal chimney of one of the large green tents, though I don't see or hear anyone nearby. As I make my way through the camp, I see a girl sitting in a Chevy sedan. The heat sounds like it's on full blast. She looks up with surprise in her eyes, but quickly returns my wave with a gloved hand and a smile. She's the first person I've seen in three days.

All morning long, even before dawn, I've seen wave after wave of geese passing overhead in a near-constant flight. I'm impressed and take it as a definitive sign of a weather change. Perhaps I might see some snow out here after all. Every time I hear the honking overhead I shake my head.

After the camp, the trail heads down into the woods, into an area noted for its waterfalls. The trail runs along and under the bluffline, which is also the fall line for all the water coming off the ridgetop. During my last hike through here, in the rain, water was pouring off nearly every overhanging ledge. If I hadn't been so cold and wet then I would've enjoyed it more.

Today, a few of the taller falls are still flowing, if only in skinny ribbons. I fill my water bottle from one of them, and after adding iodine the water looks like sweet tea. Scarcely a minute passes when I don't think about food.

The upside to the cold weather is that it reduces any temptation to linger and relax by the falls. I'm cold and on a mission today. The urge to knock of miles pulls me onward, though I would very much like to return in better weather and explore this area.

In fact, an ideal way to do this trail is to take a month

on it. Do five miles a day on the trail and spend the rest of the day off of it. There are parts of the trail where you could spend weeks exploring. But that's the problem with exploration: the more you see, the more you realize that there's a lot more to see.

I'm fortunate that I can get my year's worth of work into five or six months. With wildfires burning mainly in the summer, I have much of the rest of the year free to do what I want. My operating costs are low: my truck is paid off, I don't have a mortgage or kids, and the rent out here is free. The only price to being in nature is putting in the legwork to get out there. If you're willing.

After crossing another road, the trail begins a descent into the next drainage. The guide says it's Lynn Hollow, but I don't remember it from before—and I have a good memory. This area must've been logged a long time ago, because the trees are mostly mature here, thick and tall.

As I near the bottom, I am pleasantly surprised to see what a beautiful little hollow this is: a gentle stream flowing over smooth gray stones and big beeches looming overhead. There is an old wooden sign with "Lynn Hollow" carved into it that I like very much, certainly more than the brown carsonite posts. There are few of these wooden signs left, most having succumbed to weather and rot.

The trail follows a side drainage before passing another trickle of a waterfall. None of this seems familiar. I must've really had my head down on my last visit. After another gentle climb I reach the top of the ridge. The trees open up here, letting that cold wind back in. Ahead I see two figures in blaze orange, and facing away, they don't see me.

Here I cross I major forest road, one that is much wider and in better condition than most of the others. Near the crossing two cars are parked, one with Texas plates, the other from Oklahoma. Other hikers? I make my way over to the trail register and nose through the cards.

Behind me, I hear an ATV approaching. One of the hunters I just saw is driving, and he waves me down as he pulls into the small parking lot. He greets me with a brown-stained smile, a large wad of chew packed in his cheek. Though I have no recent deer sightings to speak of, we talk for a while. I ask if he's heard a weather forecast, but all he knows is that it got down to twenty degrees at his place last night (wherever that is), and it's supposed to be colder tonight. With a concerned look on his face he asks if I stayed warm last night, and I assure him that I'm well-prepared. As we part ways I wish him luck and he hopes I stay warm. I tell him I'll build a fire, which he approves with a nod and takes off down the road.

Not far down the way I stop at a mile marker to piss. Another hunter, along with his young son, appear right behind me as I finish, startling me. Luckily I'm all squared away so I don't expose myself when I turn towards them. We speak briefly before I'm off again, wishing them luck. I'm grateful for the human contact.

By eleven o'clock I've made eleven miles. The terrain ahead will slow me down, but I think twenty miles is definitely doable. I feel good and the double socks are keeping my feet in good shape. I still wonder if any of the cars I passed were hikers, and briefly fantasize about coming into their camp, a big fire roaring and a hot bowl of soup waiting on me. As I descend further into the drainage I finish my sweet tea water, and dream of the sensuous sound of hot tea pouring from a pot into a porcelain mug, with lots of milk and a hunk of sharp cheddar cheese and saltines to go with it.

And a fresh-baked brownie. Ah, the fantasies of hunger and privation.

An old road serves as the trail for the last jaunt down to Lewis Prong Creek. I remember this area well, and I'm glad to see the water isn't the turbid torrent I feared. Rather it is a beautiful hue of milky green. I find some rocks downstream from the crossing that look sturdy, and I use them to hop across the creek.

The tea, cheese, and brownie fantasy have caught up with me now, and I'm famished. I find a flat rock nearby and sit down, but it's so cold on my bum that I opt for the leaves instead. The stillness of sitting and the drink of cold water chill me, so I'm back on my feet in five minutes.

For the next two and a half miles the trail follows another old road, doing a bit of climbing but still gentle enough that I maintain a three mile an hour pace. The upper two creek crossings are uneventful, and despite the fresh ATV tracks I neither see nor hear anyone else. No gunfire, either. I suppose the cold weather is keeping the deer down in their beds this morning, and they won't be venturing out much today.

● ● ●

From here, it's a good grunt up into Waterfall Hollow. I'm starting to feel the fatigue setting in: I've come over fifteen miles and plan to do about seven more before I call it a day. And with two climbs ahead of me, seven miles seems like a long ways to go.

Further up the hollow, I cross an old road. I recall camping near here several years ago on the last day of winter. It had rained all day and into the night, making for a grim day of hiking. The next morning, the first day of spring, was initially dreary until I started hiking. As if to celebrate the arrival of a new season, the sun broke through and burned off the clouds, turning it into a beautiful, perfect day.

Perfect, that is, until I developed a case of food poisoning, and left a trail of diarrhea and vomit as far off the trail as I could.

I shudder at the memory and hope for better luck this time. Though the weather has been cold, cloudy, and windy, my stomach feels fine, if a bit empty. I trudge onwards.

The trail works its way up to the head of the hollow, contrary to what I remember. But I follow the white blazes, which are more reliable than my memory. Later on I realize that the trail has been rerouted here, running right up to one of the hollow's namesakes: a thin stream of water falling fifteen feet over the layered sandstone cliff. I pause and splash a bit of cold water on my face before moving on.

As I go around the next bend I see a large bird sitting in a tree just up the trail. I stop and watch it for a minute, trying to figure out what it is. It's in a bunch of branches, so I can't quite make out the plumage, but a distinct *hooooo* immediately identifies it. I slowly pick my way forward to get a better view of the owl, which lets me approach to within seventy-five feet. From here I can see it well, and the eerie yellow eyes seem to be staring right through me. A chill goes up my spine. But it doesn't seem to like what it sees, and with a silent swoop disappears deeper into the woods.

Soon I come to another waterfall, about the same size as the last. I take the last few ounces of water and pour it into a pouch containing a powdered milkshake mix. With almost 500 calories of energy, it's just what I need to get me through the next hour or two. Though I make a mess of it, I manage to get most of it down. I wish I could lay down and feel it fill my belly, but it's too cold to stop for long. I climb over the spray-slickened boulders to fill my water bottle, getting my pants soaked in the process. Can't be helped, though—I need the water.

Working my way around the flanks of Moonhull Mountain, I pass one more waterfall, though I'm so cold I barely notice. Then comes the real climbing, another grunt to the top. I'm on the west side of the ridge, the windward side, and exposed to the cold wind blowing from the northwest. It is miserable, but I have no choice but to suck it up and keep going.

When I reach the top, I run across the flat dirt road and down to the lee side. It feels better almost instantly. I still have energy from the milkshake, and the bitter wind is no longer chilling me to the core. I estimate about three and a half miles to where I want to camp.

As I hike down into Hignite Hollow, I notice the clouds above starting to thin, but there's still not a shred of blue to be seen. When I reach the creek in the bottom I don't even pause, but simply march across it and up into the woods beyond.

For the last climb of the day I swallow a mouthful of Emergen-C with some water to give me enough energy to make it up and over Brushy Ridge. The climb isn't that long or high, but it is the steepest of the day. Climbs always feel steeper later in the day.

When I reach the top I breathe a sigh of relief. The uphill is done for the day. The dirt road up here has been gated shut, and would make a nice campsite if I had enough water. From here it's two more miles downhill to Boomer Branch.

As I descend, it dawns on me that I'm going to make it—my biggest hiking day ever. The last stretch goes by in a haze, my mind fogged from fatigue and hunger. All I can think of is getting to camp and having tea and a snack.

Before long I can see the creek below me, and I'm down to the last mile. The rocks in the trail twist my ankles as I walk over them, but I manage to avoid a sprain. For the first time in many miles I notice that my feet aren't hurting at all. The double-sock idea worked, thank goodness.

Finally the trail leaves the hillside and drops down towards the creek bottom. While looking ahead, I slip on some leaves, but catch myself with a feat of quickness that I hadn't thought possible at this stage of the game. I scare up several whitetails on the bench overlooking the creek, and soon find a small, flat place to bed down. It's twenty after four and I've covered twenty-two miles. I'm done hiking for the day.

Before succumbing to the temptation to sit and rest a while, I quickly do all my camp chores. With the tarp set, water bottles full, and kitchen arranged, I grab a protein bar from my bag and sit down for a long rest.

The thrill of my accomplishment overcomes my fatigue, and I have tea with a giddiness that borders on the ridiculous. I sing and dance around camp, stretching my legs before they get too stiff. My memory had failed me here: I thought this area was more open and had a well-established campsite, but the only fire ring I find hasn't been used in some time. But no matter, it's home for the night.

The air is bitterly cold. Taking off my gloves is uncomfortable. Up above, the depressing clouds are dissolving in the sunset. I walk back to the tarp and bundle up in my sleeping bag to watch the twilight come on. Off in the distance I hear a motor groan—it seems that no matter where I camp, I can always hear a vehicle somewhere.

When I came into camp and set down my pack, the thought occurred to me that something was missing. I was mystified, as all my essential gear was with me. Now it occurs to me: *the orange vest that was on my pack.* The last time I remember seeing it on my pack was at my nine o'clock break this morning. I had taken it off to get into one of the side pockets on my pack, and now I figure that I must've left it behind the log I'd been sitting on. So, after all the little bits of hunter and hiker detritus that I've picked up, I've left behind the most visible piece of gear that I brought. But at least it's a few less ounces I have to carry over these hills. I hope the blue backpack will sufficient to ward off any target-seeking hunters. In the meantime, no wearing my brown rain jacket while hiking.

The twilight is nearly gone, and the slow emergence of the stars captivates me, providing far more enjoyment than the book. I've always been something of a stargazer and amateur astronomer, so I pick out the stars that I know. As I gaze, I recall the memory from my boyhood of peering through a telescope at the fuzzy glow of Haley's Comet. The last time it had appeared before that, Mark Twain was in his last year—a random thought that surfaces among the memories of the day.

The air seems to be warming now, or at least doesn't

seem near as cold as it was earlier. I've noticed this phenomenon many times, though whether it's actually the passage of the initial wave of cold air down the valley or just my body acclimatizing, I don't know. The wonderful feeling of warmth has become so strong I have to unzip my jacket.

For supper tonight it's the hiker's Old Faithful: macaroni and cheese, two boxes' worth. As it boils I fantasize about all the things I'd like to have with, but have to catch myself. When ready, it's the biggest and most calorie-packed meal I've had on the trail, not to mention the most delicious. I need it.

It takes me only half an hour to eat it, and with all that new fuel, my internal furnace is really burning. I take off my gloves and admire the nearly empty pot before me, using my spoon and hands to get the last bits of cheese sauce. I go down to the creek to get some water for washing, and return to camp to clean up. The stars are nearly bright enough to see by, but with all the rocks in the trail I use my headlamp, just in case.

Feeling revived, I spend an hour reading to keep my mind limber. I hear a splash down by the creek and turn of my light and listen. Nothing. A few pages later I hear footsteps coming closer, and quickly turn off the light out again. I don't see anything. Whatever it is, it is moving closer, so close that I can hear it breathing. The tension is becoming unbearable. Is it a bear?

When I turn my headlamp back on, I see two green eyes shining back. At first I can only make out a vague brown form, but as soon as the animal lifts its head I can see the long, smooth brown neck. No bear, just another deer. It soon takes off into the darkness.

Full of adrenaline, I read for another half hour before turning in. Tomorrow is a big day of a different sort: I'll re-stock from my cache about four miles up the trail, the psychological halfway point at 85.7 miles. The 90-mile mark is the true halfway point, and will mark the longest continuous distance I have ever hiked. I might take a shorter day to compensate for today, although if the weather is good and I feel fine I'll just hike till I'm tired.

Under a crystal clear moonlit sky, I go to sleep and dream of sunshine.

6

During the night I'm awakened from a deep sleep to feel a rustle at my feet. I pray that it's not a skunk coming to join me for the rest of the night. I slowly move my feet and look down to see what it is, but can't see it. I hear tiny feet patter in the leaves—a mouse. To give it a good scare I lift my legs and give the ground a good thump.

Minutes later the mouse is back again, and I can feel it nibbling on my bivy sack. The bastard. I thrash my feet and scare it off again. This time I leave my legs suspended, so if it returns I can smash it. I'm wide awake now and bent on revenge for disturbing my sleep. It doesn't take long. I hear it creep back up and let it gnaw for a few seconds before dropping my legs as hard as I can. A miss! But it did the trick, as it doesn't bother me again for the rest of the night.

The next time I open my eyes the moon is nearly behind the ridge to the west, meaning it's almost time to get up. Though I normally take off my watch and set it near my head to hear it, this time I've left it on my wrist, which is deep and warm inside my sleeping bag. I drift off again, and the light wakes me around six-thirty. I carefully crawl out of my bag, careful not to disturb the heavily bowed ceiling of my tarp. It is thickly coated with frost, the frozen condensation of my sleeping breath.

The water in the two liter bottle is mostly slush, but I manage to get enough liquid out of it for a decent-sized cup of tea. My small water bottle also feels frozen. It was a cold night, indeed.

Though there's no real need to hurry today, the thought of a whole new supply of snacks motivates me to get moving. That, and the frigid temperature. Right away the trail crosses the creek and climbs up the opposite hill. The exertion brings back feeling into my hands and toes. The sky is mostly clear, and I can see the sunlight on the hillside across the valley. It looks warm and inviting, but it'll be a while before I can get to it.

It does take a while, but out of the shade and into the light I hike, coming alongside a thick stand of pines warming in the sun. The birds are out in force, singing softly in the trees. I can finally take off my beanie and put on my lucky visor. If the day keeps warming, it will be a great day to be out here hiking. The trail on top is flat and winding, and off to the left I can see the next drainage I'll cross: the upper Mulberry River.

An enterprising hunter has put up a tree stand right beside the trail nearby, though from the look it of it, it hasn't seen use in quite a while. I admire the hunter's sense of aesthetics: in leaf-off the view through the trees over the headwaters of the Mulberry is a grand one. I contemplate climbing up into the stand, but the rusty nails, rotted wood, and possibility of tetanus dissuade me.

Walking on, the trail soon dives off the ridgetop as it descends to the river. I recall hiking this section with Dad several years ago, and he was so distracted by the scenery that we got off trail. It's difficult to miss the trail tread and blazes, but somehow we did. That's how pretty this area is.

Even in the sunlight, the air is distinctly colder in the river bottom. Frost blooms dot the side of the trail all the way to the river crossing. I look both up- and downstream to see if there are any possibilities for rock-hopping, but it is apparent that my only option here is to ford it, a grim task this frigid morning. I put my sandals on amongst the frosty leaves and walk through the icy green water. I'm up to my knees and the shock evokes an involuntary yelp. I make the last three feet to the other shore in a single leap.

Back on dry land, I stomp my feet and jog short stretches to get feeling back into my numb feet. It's a painful, but short process. Still, my fate is far luckier than the hiker who drowned here fourteen years ago, almost to the day. He was thru-hiking in his seventies—a most admirable feat. Too bad the swollen river took him. As far as I know he is the only fatality in the twenty-seven year history of the trail, but still one too many.

Once my socks and boots are back on, I continue on, crossing a forest road. Here begins the grunt up to Ozone, and my memories of this section are not pleasant because I was so nauseated from food poisoning when I last hiked here. I have little recall of the actual trail, just my numerous trips off of it.

After an initial steep section, the grade becomes more gentle. Thinking of the snacks that await in my cache at the top, I belt out Hank Williams' "Hey Good Lookin" at top volume, full of joy. That should scare away any deer or hunters. Further on I quiet down again, content to hear the music in my head. Part of my elation is the fact that my pack is the lightest it's been so far. It must be down to under thirty pounds. It makes the walking that much more pleasurable.

The thousand feet of elevation gain pass quickly, and the silence of the morning forest is broken by the roar of semis on the highway, which is just out of sight. I see a trail register and parking area just ahead, and as usual, thumb through the cards looking for others. No new ones except for Lucas's since I was here a week ago. A week ago. It seems like much longer. But only looking at my watch a few times a day has skewed my sense of time, or perhaps returned it to its natural state.

There are no cars parked at this trailhead, which means I might very well have the wonderfully scenery of the upcoming miles all to myself. But first I have to restock.

• • •

A week ago I placed my supplies in an orange five-gallon bucket and left it about a hundred yards from the trailhead, in a thick stand of pine. For good measure, I placed it in a brown garbage bag behind a large downed branch and put some pine needles on top. I figured the garbage bag would mute the bright orange color and keep any moisture out, in case the rubber seals failed.

A subtle, yet constant concern of mine has been that with all the hunters out and about, somebody has stumbled on it, possibly pilfering it or otherwise messing with it. As I go looking for it, I cannot see it, though I can see tracks in the area. Any supply problems now will cut short my trip, an unbearably grim prospect. But I soon see that my camouflage job worked better than I thought, and soon find my cache completely undisturbed, even by the squirrels.

I take off my pack with a flourish, enjoying the lightness for the last time in a while. I take out my food bags and organize small piles around the can, being careful to separate all the trash out to put in the cans at a nearby campground. Looking at the supply of bagged suppers, I have to make a decision: do I take seven and likely have one left over, or take six and risk running short if weather or something else slows me? I have 95 miles to go. I take six. I also change into a clean set of clothes—the next best thing to a shower.

After dropping in my dirty clothes and refilling my small shaker of Gold Bond body powder, I re-cover the cache can. I then hoist my provision-heavy pack onto my back and head for the trail.

The added weight is a remarkable change, but still doesn't seem as heavy as when I started. I had hoped to find something big and heavy to get rid of, but the only thing I could come up with was a change of clothes. That's the problem with experience: there aren't as many surprises.

Many times I have driven by this highway crossing, slowing to look for hikers and to catch a glimpse of the trail itself. I'd hope to see hikers, especially thru-hikers near here, thumbing a ride to the burger joint a few miles down the road, but so far I never have.

Now, as I cross the pavement, there is no sign of the semis that regularly run this route, nor any cars. Just the empty highway. On the other side I take a spur trail to the campground to drop off my trash. Before I throw away the last sugary bits of my old cereal, I eat as much as I can stand before emptying the dregs into the trash. The weight savings aren't big, but I don't want to carry any extra weight for the next 95 miles. For that matter, even another mile.

The resupply and trash dump took me just over an hour. During that time, the air has warmed up enough for me to hike in a t-shirt and light pants. With the sun shining down on me, I feel strong heading into the second leg of the hike: I've got all the food I need, I've got a good daily routine, and my feet and legs are taking the punishment well. I've even trimmed a bit of fat from my waist.

From Ozone the trail goes into the Little Piney drainage, turning into a nice creekside walk once it reaches the bottom. It's hard to believe that this time yesterday I was bundled up and freezing, praying for the wind to stop. Now, striding along in the sunlight, I begin to sweat. I also note that the ice is no longer clinking in my water bottle. Though the trail occasionally wanders out of sight of the creek, it's never out of earshot. I stop to listen to it in the distance as the birds sing overhead. Even they seem to be celebrating the sunshine.

At one of the creek crossings I go a little further upstream, where there are more rocks to hop across on. On the other side is a short, steep bank that I'm sure I can scramble up. But on the last few stones I start to wobble, ruining my momentum and sending me sprawling halfway up the bank. I reach unsuccessfully for a handhold, and slide back down into the creek. Once my feet hit the creek bottom I push off as hard as I can, springing further up the bank and catching a hold of a sapling that somehow holds all my weight.

    As I stand up, I see that my chest and legs are a muddy mess, but somehow water didn't get down into my boots. A minor miracle, though my fresh clean shirt and pants didn't last long. The bank, though, looks much worse for wear, with furrows from where my arms and legs dug in. To cover them up, I gather up some leaves and sticks and drop them on the bank. Next time, I'll just change into my damn sandals to cross.

As the miles pass underfoot, I get excited about reaching the halfway point at mile marker 90. But the last bit of the trail alongside the creek is inviting, so I find a place to sit in the sun and have a snack. Like nearly all the creeks in the Ozarks, the Little Piney runs an emerald green, due to the dissolved calcium carbonate in the water from a layer of limestone that runs through these mountains.

As I eat under the pines, I am tempted to strip down for a swim in the creek. But, seeing that I still haven't made even nine miles yet today and it is after noon, I hold off. There are two pools that I know of further along the trail that would certainly feel good after a few more miles, so I put my pack back on and head up the trail. The trail soon crosses a dirt road and begins to climb up a small hill, and the halfway point is not far.

In the years since my last visit, I see that a section of private land just down the trail has been logged, and an adjoining section of Forest Service land has been burned. The latter doesn't look as bad as it sounds; in fact, the forest looks good here, free of underbrush and plenty of open space between trees. It looks far better than the clearcut.

Finally, the magic milepost comes into view. I celebrate by stopping for a piss and a picture. The sun seems so bright I have to squint under my sunglasses. Though happy, I feel a major reality check coming on. I've hiked for six days now, including today, and I'm only halfway. That's a lot of ground still to cover, and a lot of things to go wrong in those miles, too. And since Lucas five days ago, I still haven't seen another hiker.

On the other hand, some of the prettiest country on the trail is in the next thirty miles, including some real, honest-to-God-U.S. Government-sanctioned wilderness. Why worry? No bills, no meetings to attend, no calls to make, no job to go to.

My job now is simply walking. I'm not getting paid to do this, at least in monetary terms, nor do I have to pay any entrance fees, camping fees, or permit fees. I don't have to worry about money. I have an emergency stash in my pack, but don't plan to use it. There's no store easily accessible from the trail, anyway.

Just walk, eat, sleep. Repeat. It's that simple. That's as complicated as my life gets, for now. Good.

As I hike on, the trail passes under a ridiculously low power line. I could reach up and touch it if I wanted to, but have no desire to do so. I can only imagine what would happen if a whitetail buck with a full rack came through here.

According to my stomach it's getting close to lunchtime, so I plan to fill my water bottle at the next creek and hike thirty minutes till the water is good. If my stomach lets me.

At the creek, I fill up the bottle and drop the tablets in.

Just doing that simple task, I can feel my energy bottoming out. Even the short, gentle climb out of the creek bottoms seems difficult. I need calories.

After the longest thirty minutes of the trip, I finally pull over under a large black oak. I sit still for a minute before digging out my lunch. I figure now would be a good time to dry out the tarp, so I grab the stuffsack and start spreading it out. It is quite wet, and I am surprised to see thin, white lumps in the bag, like spider eggs. I don't realize what they are till I touch one: little balls of frost, still frozen despite the warmth outside. They won't stay frozen long. I then find my tortillas and peanut butter and sit down to eat.

Lunch takes me from a lack of energy to a lack of motivation in less than thirty minutes. I just want to laze in the sun. I consult the guide to figure out a plan for the rest of the afternoon. Cedar Creek Pool is about seven miles away, and has good scenery, good campsites, and good water there. By my watch it's one-thirty, so I can get there with a bit of light left if I can keep pace.

So I put away my now-dry tarp, take a big swig of water, and head on down the trail. No rest for the lazy.

Since the resupply this morning, the weight of the pack

has been wearing on me. Though my shoulders and hips feel more tender, it's my thighs that are protesting the loudest. A dull ache beats in my quads—the fatigue from the past two days is mounting. I don't think it's bad enough yet to take a long break or take ibuprofen, just muscles playing out as the afternoon wears on.

For distraction I focus on my other preoccupation: food. Even though I'm at least a week out from finishing, I make use of the time to start planning the menu for when I do leave the woods. The first option, of course, is steak with a steaming-hot baked potato and lots of butter, macaroni and cheese, rice pilaf, homemade bread with even more butter, and chocolate ice cream for dessert.

The second option is a black bean burrito, rolled up with sharp cheddar cheese and lots of hot sauce, with a side of spicy Mexican rice and, let's say, a tall boy of Tecate to wash it down with, and more waiting in the fridge with plenty of limes. All afternoon I torture myself this way, adding little refinements here and there in a hopelessly hungry fantasy world.

To tackle the pack weight problem I dig out some fig newtons before they disintegrate into a lumpy, crummy mess.

They taste unbelievably good, and I imagine them topped with whipped cream.

After slogging along in my food-filled haze, I descend into the Lick Creek drainage, ready for a break. I cross the pleasant stream and drop my pack at the foot of the next climb. It's time for a snack and a side trip.

I walk upstream on an old jeep road for a few hundred yards until I see the familiar spot. There's an immensely inviting swimmin' hole with a beautiful little waterfall. The creek has carved a smooth slot through the overhanging rock, giving this lovely spot the name "Slot Rock". I cross the narrow span at the top of the waterfall to get a better view of the other side.

After I load up on more fig newtons and trail mix, I test the temperature of the pool: very cold. And though the air is warm, the shadows are getting longer and there are few places to dry in the sunshine. My tired mind is conflicted: I have four miles to go to Cedar Creek, but it will be near dark when I get there at the rate I'm going. I also want to stay here and swim, but it would be a chilly experience indeed.

Instead of making a decision, I lay back and gaze at the blue sky and listen to the water run and whisper in the creekbed. A place more peaceful would be hard to find. My belly gurgles happily with food, and my eyelids grow heavy…

I snap awake after several minutes of half-sleep, and feel much better. I decide to hoof it to Cedar Creek, so I take an Emergen-C to get me through the last leg and check my guide one last time before setting out. I spend a long few moments admiring Slot Rock before setting off again.

On the elevation chart in my guide, the next climb looks deceitfully easy, so I march lightly back to my pack and start up. Even though the trail follows an old road here, the grade is tough. Another steep afternoon climb. But the highest waterfall on the trail is just ahead so I have something close to look forward to.

The trail levels out and on a nearby tree I see a blue blaze that marks a spur trail to a small overlook in the creek just below the main trail. This is the place for the waterfall, but it is dry. So much for that.

Looking up the hill, I scan the trail, seeing where it has been built into the side of the steep slope with rocks. It goes up and up—not just steep, but awful. As I plod onwards I decide it's the worst climb on the trail so far. Four miles to camp suddenly seems much more distant in the waning light of the afternoon. I start to wonder if I should've called it a day back at Slot Rock—I could be stretched out on the ground making tea right now if I'd have stopped. But I silence those thoughts after a few moments; they do me no good. Besides, it's barely three o'clock and though my energy is low, it is steady.

Eventually the climb eases up, though it is still gaining elevation. The forest is open here, full of afternoon sunshine. My mood improves even more after I pass mile marker 96, where the path flattens out and the walking becomes more of a stroll in the woods. The sunshine is tonic for my tired soul.

Feeling stronger, I cross the ubiquitous forest road on top, which also signals the end of the uphill. Now the roller-coaster trail is heading back down. Only two miles to go. I reluctantly pass into shadow, likely the last sunshine I'll feel till sometime tomorrow morning, a depressing thought. But even in the shade the air still feels nice. I hope it doesn't get too cold down in Cedar Creek tonight.

Even though the scenery here is beautiful, especially as I hit another stand of beeches, it seems more abstract, distant. I can only think of rest, hot tea, and food. I sing some more

Hank Williams to buoy my mood, trying to remember all the words to "Settin' the Woods on Fire".

Soon I get my first look down into Cedar Creek. I'm getting close, and the walking is now level. I pass through another stand of pines, sweetening the afternoon air. Still up high in the drainage, I take a quick pause to take in the scenery. I try to pinpoint where tonight's camp might be, but the woods seem to go on forever from here. The sunlight has made it halfway up the opposite ridge.

More trail, old roadbeds, and more downhill. There's always more. When I pass milepost 98 I know I have don't have that much further, maybe ten minutes of hiking. The end is near. A pretty ravine opens up on the left as I finish the last of the descent, another one that deserves a closer look. I try to imagine it in the spring, bedecked with green, but the half-light down here makes it look dark and mysterious this afternoon.

The creek is flowing strong when I reach it just beyond the ravine. I find a good spot to cross, and make it across in much better fashion than my attempt earlier in the day. I follow another old road, which I recognize will take me right into camp. I halfway hope to see a curl of smoke ahead, fellow hikers gathered around a campfire. But the other part of me hopes for another quiet night of solitude, and that part gets its wish I stroll into the campsite at Cedar Creek Pool around four-thirty.

It's too cold to swim now, but that does nothing to diminish the beauty of the pool. It's the kind of place that needs a rope swing, and I can easily see myself spending hours here on a warm day. The deep emerald of the water is incredibly beautiful, almost tropical, like the ocean off the sandy beaches of the Caribbean. I'm glad I pushed through to make it here. Now all that slogging this afternoon suddenly seems worth it.

The peace of the Ozark evening quickly settles over camp. The air is cool and quiet while the stream sings its liquid song. My camp chores are done, and I feel a resurgence of energy: the excitement of being in a beautiful place with the satisfaction of having hiked a long ways to get there.

Checking my guide, I find I covered nearly seventeen miles today. No wonder I felt so tired coming up the other side of the ridge this afternoon. That makes over 38 miles the past two days, bumping my daily average to over sixteen miles. I'll hike a shorter day tomorrow.

Just like Fane Creek camp several days ago, this is a well-established and well-used campsite. The scenery and the flat ground make it ideal. I wonder if there was ever a homestead here; it's good ground for it. The old fire ring, full of old campfire ashes, has been covered with flat rocks, which makes it a knee-high table—perfect for cooking. A new fire ring has been built a few feet away, but I feel no need to use it right now. Instead of my usual routine of laying under the tarp with tea and a snack, I sit here, eating and reading and enjoying the last light of the day.

With my boots off and sandals on, my feet are recovering well from another day of pounding, especially after I washed them in the cold creek water. A few small birds flutter near the pool, but otherwise there is no sound—not even a vehicle or gunshot to be heard.

Twilight brings on the last flurry of activity from the birds and squirrels as I turn my attention back to the book. Despite the intrigue in the book, I feel very peaceful. Star-rise captures my attention back from the book as the cool, dark night comes on.

For a break I take a walk down the old roadbed, enjoying the open view of the heavens as I amble along. Leaves crunch underfoot at every step.

The only other time I've been here was with a group, and boisterous one at that. It was an organized outing with folks from all over western Arkansas. We were out for an overnight backpack on this section. After supper the obligatory bottle of whiskey made the rounds around a blazing campfire. And though I miss the companionship, I don't feel that being alone out here has diminished the experience in any way. It has brought me that much closer to the heart of it.

After a supper of creamy noodles, I treat myself to a hot cup of spiced apple cider I'd stored in the resupply can for just such an occasion. Pouring the steaming water into the mug and powdered cider mix produces an aroma that borders on the sensual. I instantly feel warmer. I take my time drinking it, enjoying the starshine and satellites streaking silently overhead. The moon doesn't rise till I have already put my things away for the night and am snug in my bag.

Going over the mileage figures for the trail ahead, I

figure I have four or five nights left, depending on weather, physical condition, etc. I know I want to take it easy the next two days, since I'll be in the most rugged and sublime country on the trail. After that, I'll just see how much I feel like hiking. I just hope my folks will be able to get my truck to the end of the trail before I do.

    Tomorrow is the day I've been looking forward to the most since I started: the Hurricane Creek Wilderness. Most hikers simply call it the Hurricane. Though it was one of the first sections of this trail that I hiked, I can still remember it vividly and with great fondness. I was there in time for the height of the fall colors, one of the most spectacular displays I've ever seen. Though I've already passed that time this fall, I know the scenery alone will be incredible. And that's what I came out here to see.

7

The night passes quickly during the most undisturbed sleep I've yet had on the trail. The magic of the morning wakes me early, just after first light but long before the dawn. It is the best time to be in the woods, before the sun's brush paints this autumn forest a pale gold. The birds are up, too, and I can hear their morning songs sweeten as the sun comes.

Sleep has driven the fatigue from my legs and mind, as if I've already had my morning tea. There's no frost this morning, making it easier to emerge from my sleeping bag. Only the very brightest of the stars remain visible in the clear sky as I walk down to my stove and set the water to boil.

While waiting, I walk over to the creek to breathe the

sharp scent of the cedars that line the banks. It's early and the day already has a good feel.

When the water's ready I put in the tea and powdered milk, then finish putting my bedding away. Picturing the scenery that awaits me, I work quickly, with purpose. While packing I grab handfuls of mini-wheats to speed up packing and breakfast time.

After putting away my stove and cooking gear, I take one last walk down to the creek and pool. The soft, early light makes for pretty reflections in the water, but too dark to photograph with my camera. I then turn and head up the trail, right into a climb. It's just after seven.

The going up is steady but slick, particularly on the steep, leafy sections. As usual, it takes me several minutes to warm up, even hiking hard. I'm glad I stopped where I did yesterday; this would've been tough late in the day. My feet feel like they completely recovered from the past two lengthy days of hiking, and are not bothered by the numerous rocks on the trail.

At the top of the climb I cross the usual road, having made the first mile in about twenty-five minutes. That's the pace I'm shooting for, especially on the uphills. I'm glad I was able to maintain it, despite the added weight of the resupply.

I come out of the shadow into hazy sunlight—high clouds above and gunmetal gray clouds off to the north. I hope it passes, but can't do anything about it. I would love to have good weather when I'm in the Hurricane.

Around milepost 100 I feel I can finally stop and strip off my long underwear. I take a snack break to load up on more cereal and keep my energy up. 100 miles: now that's a psychologically satisfying number. The thought of hiking that far gives me a big shot of confidence, one that I hope will last for the rest of the hike.

The trees in this area are thinner than the surroundings, so there's a great view down into Gee Creek Valley just below, and Haw Creek Valley to the east. Pines are scattered on the ridgetops, which is typical of the Ozarks, as they tend to grow in drier places. The scattered stands are the only green thing I can see from here.

As I work my way downstream into Gee Creek, I can see the remains of the old homestead in this area. A rock wall lines the north bank of the creek for a long stretch, though the forest has reclaimed much of the bottomland. Vines, thick brush, and trees about where once was grown cotton, corn, potatoes, and anything else a settler could make a go of. For the solitary settler, this would be a most remote place. Even now it is in one of the most remote places in the state: the middle of nowhere, just where I like to be.

The trail continues to work its way downstream and finally crosses Gee Creek, staying in the woods the whole time. The air here is thick and humid, chilling me to the bone. I sure wish the sun was out.

Occasionally I can hear the roar of a semi down on Highway 123, the next road crossing. As the trail drops down towards the road, I recall the only other time I've hiked here. It was a painful descent for me that time, as I'd developed an ugly blister on my left heel and had hiked ten miles on it that day. Somehow I was able to limp all the way to the trailhead, where I took off my boots to see that the blister had spread to the entire heel. I made sure to upgrade my socks and footwear after that disaster.

This time is much better. Nothing hurts and the sun soon comes out. In fact, the high clouds appear to be thinning out, allowing more light through. The sound of another semi rumbles through the forest as I reach a trail register. After another fruitless check through the cards, I continue on down to the campground on Haw Creek.

After crossing the highway the trail stays on pavement, crossing a concrete low water bridge and through one loop of the Forest Service campground. The creek is high enough to run over the top of the low water bridge, but is spread so thin that the tops of my boots stay dry.

As soon as I reach the other side I see a large, fast Boxer sprinting towards me, a hunter orange handkerchief tied around his neck. Ever since I had several bad encounters with dogs in Ecuador two years ago I've been much more wary around strange dogs. This one is so full of energy he scarcely pauses to jump on me, then does laps around me, wagging his little bobbed tail.

The dog's owners are just ahead, camped in a small trailer just outside the campground gates. They turn to see the dog and I drawing near, and give the dog a call while waving generously to me. They say the dog isn't dangerous, though he is starting to annoy me to death. He just won't back off. They call out to him again, but he stays right with me.

I pass by the trailer and keep going, but the dog seems ready to come along with me. As he comes up in front of me, he suddenly jumps and puts his paws on my chest. I'm startled, but can see the playfulness in his eyes, and finally pet him. He's not the fierce guard dog I'd feared and keeps begging for more attention. I keep walking.

From behind I hear the high, awful whine of an ATV, and the dog's owner comes blazing down the wrong way of the one-way road to get him. Just in time, too—I need to dump last night's trash and don't want a dog around when I pull out my food bags.

Looking around, I see there are a few occupied sites in the campground, but not many people around. I suppose many are still out hunting.

A short walk across the campground brings me to a lovely waterfall, naturally named Haw Creek Falls. I set my pack on one of the huge slabs of stone, above the high-water line, and slide down another slab to the foot of the falls. Though only a four-foot drop, the water pours off a wide shelf of rock. There isn't much water falling this time, as spring is the ideal time to see it, but it still is a peaceful place to sit a while. I take a few minutes to daydream. The view upcreek towards the ridge I just descended is a pleasant one.

Two women in their pajamas walk up from behind,

keeping a wide berth around this dirty, hairy hiker. They look young, at least younger than me, and after I smile and nod to them they pick their way across the rocks towards me. I'm sitting at the best view spot.

    They introduce themselves and one of them tells me that they just hiked the last twenty-mile section of the trail, starting at the last trailhead, where I restocked. She said they took two nights and "absolutely loved it". She is getting more animated as we share stories, though her friend looks much more tired. When I tell them what I'm doing, she peppers me with questions. I'm grateful for the company, and try not to talk her ear off. After more questions, she tells me about other sections of the trail she's hiked, to which I listen intently. For her, reaching Hare Mountain was an emotional experience. She cried as she took in the view, a feeling I can relate to well. It *is* beautiful.

    After a few more minutes of talk, I ask them about the weather. They don't know any more of the forecast than I do, and a quick glimpse up at the sky is all we can do.

    With a flourish of gracefulness, they tell me they better leave so I can continue my hike. I thank them and wish them well, and take a few more moments at the falls. Ready to get on to the Hurricane, I walk back to my pack and keep on.

The next white blaze is a welcoming sight as I start back into the woods. It's about a mile and a half to the next road crossing, after which the Hurricane begins. The trail is quite slick as I climb up out of Haw Creek. It's on a north aspect, so it hasn't dried out much from the last bout of rain several days ago. I stumble and slip but avoid a major wipeout. The views down into Haw Creek are lovely, and make the distance pass quickly.

I'm thankful when the trail passes into sunshine as it nears the next crossing. I pass an armadillo on the side of the trail, so engrossed in its rooting that it pays me no mind as I pass.

The light is getting brighter and temperature delightfully warmer. I wade through a mucky section, then pass some small cedars before reaching an overgrown field. An old abandoned schoolhouse appears, marking the next trailhead parking lot. I scan the post board for anything interesting, seeing an outdated notice of a trail re-route twenty miles ahead.

In the sunlight the grass of the field is a brilliant green, and I choose to walk in it for as long as I can to avoid the pavement. Up ahead is a narrow one-lane bridge and after it, the Hurricane Creek Wilderness.

Before crossing the bridge I listen for a few seconds for any possible oncoming traffic. This would not be a good place to meet a semi and have a *Stand By Me*-type experience. I sprint across and pray as I run that no trucks or cars will come around the bend while I'm on the bridge. I'd have nowhere to go but over the side, into Big Piney Creek.

Luck is with me, and no cars come as I make it to the other side of the bridge. I take a left past the bridge abutment onto an old road that marks the edge of the Wilderness. I feel an immense sense of joy as I start up into the woods, like I'm coming home. The uphill doesn't bother me.

The sun is shining brilliantly as I come alongside a pine-studded bluffline, bathed in light. I think this would be an ideal place to watch the sunrise, made even better by the beautiful view into the valley below.

At the next milepost, 107, I find a small piece of flat ground near some rocks and take a snack break. It hasn't been that long since I left Haw Creek Campground but I'm already famished. Fortunately, I've done all the climbing for the day—from here it's either on the level or downhill.

As always, the temptation to lay around, take a nap, stare at the trees, and keep eating is strong. But, the scenery is calling to me. I promise to take it slow, remembering little bits of Thoreau that praise the benefits of sauntering. Too bad he never saw the Ozarks.

Here the trail stays mostly flat, and I can feel the sun heating the air to near-spring-like temperatures. The gentle breeze through the beeches is sweet and warm. Though my shoulders and hips are sore under the straps of my pack, my legs and feet feel fit as a fiddle. I walk along mindfully, absorbed in every step. The trail seems to glide underfoot.

Before I realize it, I reach the next milepost and am drawn out of the trance. It's that same feeling of driving long distances: I'm not asleep, but everything seems to register on a different level. This type of experience is the closest I feel I can get to a still mind. The river of thoughts flows along smoothly, never stopping.

• • •

The trail continues on the level for quite a while, longer than I remember. I start feeling impatient to get down to the creek, find a camp, and take a swim. As I plod on, the wide valley of Hurricane Creek opens up through the trees to the north. As far as I know, all I can see is wilderness. This is rugged country. In most ways, it looks a lot like what I've already hiked through, but knowing that it is protected from development forever makes it look and feel that much more special.

When the trail finally begins the descent down to the creek, I jog the first hundred yards or so, just to shake things up. I look out over the valley—which is truly more of a canyon—and there is not a cloud to be seen in the noontime sky. I listen for the rush of the creek far below, but cannot tell if I'm hearing that, or the wind in the trees.

My plan is to camp about a mile or so after I cross the creek, which is still a ways down. My feet smart as I hike on the rocks, but otherwise everything else is holding up. Despite the fatigue and continual hiking, I feel my legs are getting stronger.

Through the trees I can see the giant gray boulders that litter the creek bed below the trail. I'm not far now. The sound of flowing water is thrilling. Perhaps it is some atavistic trait leftover from the primordial brain. Or just my thirst—I ran out of water a mile back.

Reaching the crossing point, I look up- and downstream to see some of the most wild, rough country in the state. The steep walls of the canyon have left car-sized boulders littered all over the creek and on the banks. The elevation of the ridges on either side is about 500 feet above me.

Here the lively look of the green-tinted water contrasts sharply with the leafless trees sullenly hanging over ashen rock of the streambed. My heart swells with joy as an involuntary smile spreads across my face. This is why I'm doing this hike: for moments like these, to be a silent witness to the backwoods beauty of my native state. I am home.

On the other side of the creek I see a wide ledge that looks like a good lunch spot. I clamber over several boulders to make it across dry—a lot of work to get across a shallow creek. The breeze feels wonderful on my sweaty back after I take off my pack. I plop down on the ledge and get out my water filter to top myself and water bottle off. I need water now and can't wait for the iodine to work. The filter is still slow from the pond muck, despite a rinse to clear out the grit, but I don't mind the work.

I sit so as to let the sun dry my back, glad for the warmth and fine weather. I pull out some food for lunch, glad to have grabbed a cheese packet (instead of the usual peanut butter) to go with my tortilla-and-a-half today. In fact, I see the cheese has bits of jalapeno in it, a real treat.

Back in my normal life, I would never touch such heavily processed and preserved stuff, but to keep going out here I need the calories. With some more experimentation I'm sure I can find better food, but haven't had the time to try out many things before this trip.

Anyway, I take my time eating, careful to extract every bit of goopy orange cheese to fill my belly and cut down on the weight of my trash. I chase the tortillas and cheese with a huge handful of cold, hard M&Ms, letting them warm up in my mouth before I chew them up. I can feel the rush of all that sugar as I pack up and get moving again.

According to the guide, it's only about three-quarters of a mile to where I want to camp. Not far at all. I reach an old pioneer road, long unused, and follow it, paralleling the creek.

On the hillside to my left a bluff rises the further I go. Soon it is at least seventy-five feet tall, with occasional rivulets of water streaking down the face.

A sign points the way to a natural bridge nearby, so I make the short excursion over to it. It's impressive how just one small stream of water falling over face has carved out the bridge. The early afternoon light is perfect, with shadows slanting to the east. I sit on a nearby rock, content to rest and admire the surfeit of scenery that abounds here.

Drifting into a daydream, I imagine the formation of the bridge, the silver stain of water becoming a waterfall of white. The trees around me swell into grandfatherly giants. It will always be beautiful.

For fifteen minutes I stay and contemplate the view. The shadows sweep across the rock, subtly shifting every passing second. I can't help but wonder why I find it so beautiful here. The uniqueness? The wilderness designation? The remoteness? Yes, and the effort to get here. I am just a visitor here. Every hiker is. The only mark of man—the road—will be washed away, leaving only this narrow thread of a moss-covered trail to show anyone was ever here.

My good fortune in having this place to myself pleases

and astounds me, though I'd be happy to share it with anyone on a day such as today. I almost feel sorry no one else is out here, experiencing all *this*.

After my fill of contemplation, I resume hiking. A narrow, but deep gash through the cliffs soon opens up on the left, and I can see a good spot to camp down the hill. I follow through the trail on, switchbacking once before I reach it. There's good flat ground, a small fire ring with stones on which to sit, and a fantastic view of Hurricane Creek here. I quickly set up camp and change into sandals before picking my way down to the creek.

A large, flat boulder juts over the creek. Between it and another boulder runs a short, swift waterfall. I've brought my book, camera, water bottle and a snack to while away the afternoon. Before reading, I test the water to see if it's warm enough for swimming. It's not. But there's a pool downstream that looks inviting, so I strip down naked and wade into the waist-high water. The frigid water is almost painful, but exhilarating. I manage to splash enough water on myself to rinse off the grime and sweat, but am soon driven back to dry ground with numb legs.

The boulder is lukewarm when I sit my wet ass down it, and I warm up in the sunshine. Before I'm all dry, I take another plunge into the pool for good measure, then retreat to the boulder to dry and get dressed. There's not enough room on the boulder to lay my whole body, so I dangle my feet over the creek and turn my back to the sun. It doesn't take long to dry, and I put my clothes back on to cover the goosebumps. I read for a while, then take a break to watch the sun disappear behind the ridge to the west.

Something about the afternoon brings on the desire for contemplation, particularly in the woods. While morning is the time to get things done, these hours are the best for simple meditation. I spend the time watching the shadows grow, and listen to the subtle voices singing from the water. The pitch of the creek flowing past a nearby boulder is high, but after tumbling over a two-foot drop it becomes a *basso profundo*, then mellows to a tenor as it flows onward.

I could sit here the rest of the day—hell, for days on end and perhaps the rest of my life trying to understand it all.

Another kind of happiness is dry gear. Back up in camp I check to see that the tarp is dry, and my sleeping bag is wonderfully light and airy. Not too aromatic, though: it smells like a wet dog that just paddled through a stock pond, despite airing it out in the afternoon sun. But like a good dog, it's been with me for years and hasn't let me down yet: a good companion.

    Everything down here is now in shadow, though there's still a good bit of daylight left. To stretch my legs I hike over to Cedar Limb Hollow, just around the bend. At first, it's hard to tell if there's a creek here, or it's just a large break in the cliff. A house-sized boulder with eastern red cedars growing atop it, dominates the entrance to the hollow. I rock hop in the creekbed, feeling the chill of the cold air and water on my feet. The air smells especially autumn-like, combining the aromas of wet leaves and moss on stone, carried by the downstream breeze.

    To get further up the hollow I climb up the left embankment, slipping and sliding on the dirt and leaves. I can't get the traction with my sandals that I can with my old boots. My feet are smarting from the cold, as well as the day's hike, so I turn around after a few minutes of exploring. Before leaving, I look up the hollow, hoping to see a better turn-around point—a waterfall, a rockfall, another boulder—but I see none and amble back to camp.

Now's a good time to stock up on water, so I fill my bottles, my cooking pot, and tea mug at the creek. After boiling water for tea in camp, I take my mug back down the creek to drink it with another snack. With the light waning, I don't get much read, but manage to spend plenty of time taking in more of the scenery. A sudden wave of down-canyon air sweeps over me, so I return to my pack to put on more layers. The temptation to slide into my bag for a nap is too much to ignore, so I lay out on my foam pad and make my bed.

As I zip up the bag I look around camp, deeming it the best campsite on the trail, and high on my lifetime list. This is a powerful place. Here in the Hurricane I feel more present than ever. Each moment I feel more alive. In my imaginings before the trip, this is how I hoped it would be. I'm a lucky man to be here.

After a short nap, I'm delighted to awaken and find myself here, that I wasn't just dreaming.

• • •

With the twilight coming on, I roll on my back to gaze up at the early evening stars. I realize that since I crossed the invisible line into the Hurricane, I haven't heard a single vehicle or gunshot. I haven't even seen any low-flying planes, which frequently buzz the ridgetops here. I feel like I have the whole of the woods to myself.

It takes me a few minutes to get my bearings in the sky. My orientation is off, because most of the drainages I've crossed run north-south, whereas here Hurricane Creek runs roughly east-west. Off to the west I see two bright stars, though I'm sure one of them has to be a planet—it has noticeably moved across the night sky in the past few weeks. My favorite part of the evening is when it gets dark enough to see shooting stars, those metallic meteors punching holes in the heavens. I watch a few satellites pass over as it gets closer to supper time, but no shooting stars yet.

The evening meal tonight is buttery, garlicky noodles. I prefer thin noodles, as they cook quicker than regular noodles, and can be eaten quicker. The flat stones are too cold to sit on bare, so I bring my foam pad over and drape it on the rock near my stove. Much better. I have to watch the pot carefully, as it tends to boil over whenever my attention is diverted. The smell is tantalizing, obscenely appetizing. They never smell this good back at my apartment in Boise.

Glancing at my watch, I realize that my girlfriend will soon be going out to a concert of one our favorite bands. She'd even bought me a ticket several months before, thinking I might be around. I miss her very much, but I don't regret being out here. For the music, I can always listen to the CD later. For this hike, there is no substitute.

I eat, clean my pot, and have everything stowed away in less than an hour. Finally getting the routine down. I sorely miss having a cup of hot apple cider like I did last night. I make a note to bring more for future trips. It's a lightweight luxury I can afford to carry.

It never ceases to amaze me how well just the starlight can illuminate the forest. Even with twilight long gone I can make out the rocks on the way down to the creek without tripping. I want one last look before calling it a night. With little other sensory input, the creek sounds bigger, as if in flood. I feel as if I could be washed away and swallowed up by the creek in any minute. But that doesn't bother me. After a faint shooting star in the east I decide to head to bed.

Since it is such a spectacular starry night, I pull my

sleeping bag and pad out from under the tarp for a better vantage. No sense in staring at blue nylon when I can enjoy a view of the whole galaxy from my bed. A bright meteor slashes across the heart of the sky, the last thing I remember seeing before I fall asleep.

8

The morning comes cold and clear, with a light frost. But the open sky holds the promise of a warm and sunny day. Moving quickly in the frigid air, I start heating the water and packing. A glance at my watch shows that it's well after seven, but there's no hurry today. It'll be another short day.

After a few minutes of sipping tea and eating cereal down by the creek, I resume packing. That'll keep me warm until the sun hits the valley. When my pack is all set to go, I make one last trip down to the creekside for a few minutes of meditation. Light clouds of vapor float above the waterfall.

Around eight-twenty I hoist my pack and take the first steps on the trail for the day. I cross the gently flowing stream of Cedar Hollow and follow the rocky trail parallel to the creek. The sunlight finally reaches down here in the bottomland, making the creek sparkle like a diamond through the trees.

It's hard to concentrate on the trail when there's so much around to look at. The sunshine slants through the forest, warming the cool morning air. Down in the shadier sections of the creek, I can see small white sheets of ice in the shallows.

I wonder if the creek can be floated in high water. I don't see why not. A kayak would be ideal because of the technical sections, though an inner tube would be more fun. Especially with a few friends and a cooler of beer.

The thought of a cooler of beer immediately sets my saliva flowing and my stomach growling. Didn't I just eat breakfast? And thinking of food, the next tributary I come to is Greasy Creek. The bottomland here is wide, and in full sun. Passing the remains of an old homestead, I see that the settlers took advantage of that to sight their buildings and crop fences in the center, allowing for a maximum amount of light. I admire their forethought.

I'm curious why it was named it Greasy Creek. Was it

their last name, or something related to their activities here, or just the first thing that came to mind? I'll never know. But I've always been interested in the history of place names ever since I learned that one of my grandfathers was born in a settlement called Skunk Hollow.

On I walk into a section of trail where the trees form a perfect canopy. The light is just right, so I stop to take a picture and admire it. The perfect trail picture. As I walk by I hold my hand out to rub one of the trees in a gesture of thankfulness. It returns the gesture with a few surprise drops of dew on my bare head.

Back along the Hurricane Creek, the trail abruptly heads left up a somewhat steep climb. The guidebook explains that this section was constructed to avoid a private inholding of property here. It's a bit taxing on the lungs and legs, but once it levels out the view is incredible. Despite a recent blowdown, the area has grown up a lot since my last time here, though not enough to obscure the view down into Hurricane Creek. And looking up, there is not a cloud to be seen in the cerulean sky.

Soon the trail heads back down towards the creek and another crossing. The trail is squarely in the sun, so I enjoy the warmth and light as I descend. Ahead I can see where upper Hurricane Creek bends to the north, and the ridge on the east side of the creek where the trail will soon take me.

The crossing of Hurricane Creek is wide, but not shallow enough to make it across dry. Despite knowing the answer, I test the water with my hand, feeling the chill immediately. But having no other option, I take of my boots and socks, change into my sandals, and splash across. The slippery rocks provide little purchase, and my right leg slides down into the water up to the knee before I can right myself. Fighting the biting cold all the way across, I make it without further incident and walk up to a primitive campsite to change footwear.

Despite the creekside location, this site is not nearly so scenic as the one I enjoyed last night. Good enough, to be sure: flat ground, good views of the creek, surrounded by lovely hills. But it lacks the dramatic heights and rushing whitewater that makes the lower section of the creek so spectacular.

There is also a dirt and gravel road that crosses the creek here, for access to the private inholding I passed earlier in the morning. Judging from the ruts, it's been some time since a vehicle passed this way. Only some faint horse tracks appear on the roadway. Even though it's in the wilderness, the landowner still has a right to access his property on the road, at least according to the guidebook.

My feet feel much better once they're warm inside my shoes and boots again. While having a snack I walk around the campsite, finding a few pieces of old trash and a pair of imitation Doc Martens in the fire ring. I imagine someone got fed up with hiking in them, and this seemed like a logical place to leave them. Unfortunately I don't have the room to pack them out—they'll have to stay. All the other trash is coming with me.

The sun hasn't yet reached this side of the creek, and won't for some time. So, I press on, hiking in the shadow of a ridge to the south. It's cool enough not to want to stop, though with the ease of the trail there's not much need to. Along the way there is an occasional view down to the creek on my left, and a few openings that allow an excellent look to the west, into the heart of the wilderness.

It seems like everywhere else in the valley the sun is shining. I'm guessing it'll be a while before I'm in it, though.

But I notice that my pack already seems a bit lighter today, not sitting so heavily on my hips. All the eating is paying off.

For one last time the trail draws along Hurricane Creek, so I fill up my water bottle before the trail starts another climb. I quietly thank the creek, then turn to head up the ridge.

After passing a spur trail to a nearby trailhead, the climb begins. In the guidebook it looks like a good grunt, and feels like it out here. The trail seems to sidehill forever, working my ankles hard.

Without knowing it, I pass the invisible line of the wilderness just before passing mile marker 119. It's been a welcome change to be in a section of land without the usual manmade intrusions. Besides man, that is. I imagine packing in enough supplies for a month, to make it through the changing of leaves. The small trailhead I just passed would make a good drop-off point. Will have to remember that.

The trail keeps climbing as it turns southeast, then south. Now I'm back in the lovely sunshine. I stumble here and there on the rocks, but my ankles are still handling the strain. They'll be sore tomorrow, I think.

About a mile further I find a good solid boulder where I have lunch. When I resupplied, I got a new brand of tortillas which I like much better than the ones I had on the first leg of the trip. I look forward to lunch more than ever. I've also remembered to put the peanut butter packet in my pocket while I hike to warm it up and make it easier to spread. This discovery, too, has improved my lunches.

For dessert I have a few fig newtons and some trail mix, providing a sugar boost for the next stretch of trail. I finish the last of my water and set off—on the map there's another creek about a mile away.

The mile passes quickly, and I am surprised that this lovely little creek is labeled "Unnamed Creek." Surely something better can be thought of than that. How about Sweet Creek? Will have to take this up with the USGS when I get out.

There is a lovely spot to camp here, especially during the longer days when the sun can reach down here. Moss covers many of the rocks around here, too.

Just one more climb and I'll be over to Buck Branch, where I'm thinking about spending the night. I've hiked about ten miles so far today, and it's only a couple more to there. The trail climbs out of Unnamed Creek, staying in the shade. Every now and then I catch a good glimpse back across the country I've covered the past two days.

After meandering through some large boulders, the trail starts dropping down to Buck Branch. From a distance it looks like the upper part—where I plan to camp—is in the sun.

After the trail reaches the creek, I find a small, flat campsite just up from the water. I happily set up the tarp in the sun and find a good tree nearby to sit under while I read. I look forward to another relaxing afternoon in the woods.

The sun disappears over the wooded ridge to the southeast an hour after I get to camp. It doesn't take long for the cool air to get to me, so I start bundling up. It's three o'clock, though hiking so much in the shade today makes me thinks it's much earlier.

Just above camp two tributaries meet to form the main body of Buck Branch, flowing surprisingly strong for this time of year. The creek bed just downstream is carved from solid rock, and moss is growing in sheets where the water seeps over the smooth embankment across from camp. It's pretty, but I miss the openness and big views of last night's camp.

Down here I feel more cramped and shut in by the terrain. The afternoon cold doesn't help, either.

After filling up on water, I decide to recon up the trail to see what awaits me first thing. Following the old roadbed (which is the trail in this area), the path climbs the nose of a ridge that separates two upstream tributaries. It gets the blood pumping, and I feel more comfortable in the cold. The feeling of walking without weight is sheer pleasure.

For afternoon tea it's a brimming mugful. My total fuel usage for the first leg of the trip was about half a liter of white gas, half of what I'd expected. So, on this leg, I'm determined to use more and get the weight's worth of hot water. It's good for morale, too, especially on these cold afternoons.

With mug in hand, I head back down the trail to check out an old bridge that was likely built during the logging days. It looks like a 20s' or 30s' era stone bridge, and has held up well, though no telling when the last vehicle actually used it. I admire the functional craftsmanship, and how well it blends in with the scenery around it.

Another old road, usable only by ATVs, runs up the hill to the south. I follow it up a ways, seeing only a faint tire track in one of the many mudholes. I doubt anyone has used it for a while, either. According to my map, it leads back up to Highway 123, the eastern part of the highway I crossed before starting into the wilderness. In the distance, near what appears to be the ridgetop, I can hear a pack of dogs barking and whining. I hope they're fenced in at someone's trailer or cabin. I'm tempted to see how far up they and the highway are, but it's getting dark and I didn't bring my headlamp.

  Feeling warm and content, I saunter back down to camp as the first stars of the night emerge overhead. I clear all the leaves from under the tarp to help pick out the rocks that might stick into me when I go to bed. When I'm finished I lay down to test it, and am disgusted by the rotten, putrid smell. I fear this area might have been used as a toilet by some hunters or other hikers, but checking around with my light I see no obvious evidence of it. Probably just the smell of the leaves decaying. I wish I'd done this earlier, though, to let it air out for a while. I hope that between now and bedtime it fades away. I'll be sure to keep my pack away from it. Perhaps I should've stayed back at Unnamed Creek.

  With a lot of time before supper, I drag my pad over to the small fire ring. I fetch my sleeping bag and book from my pack to do my evening reading. I'm just over halfway finished with the novel, so I better get busy if I want to finish it before the end of the hike. I'm at milepost 123, so I've got 57 more miles to get through 450-odd pages. Might have to take another short day to get that done, though I've had two in a row and have barely made a dent. But I'm not tired tonight, so I might just stay up to do some extra reading.

The cold air makes for brilliant nights, owing to the lack of humidity the air can hold. And tonight the sky looks especially clear and crystalline through the trees around camp. I wish it were more open to the sky—should make that a criteria of campsite selection.

After ninety minutes of Dostoyevsky my stomach is ready for food. Instead of cherry-picking a meal, I just reach in the food bag and grab one out: four-cheese noodles, though the powder hardly looks like any kind of cheese that I've ever seen. The air is bone-chilling, so I hover over the stove as the pot heats. With a light breeze blowing downstream, I turn my back to it and help shield the stove. I grab my rain jacket from my pack for an extra layer and pull the hood over my beanie. That helps a lot more than I thought it would, and I feel like I can keep warm this way.

After adding the noodle mix to the boiling water, I

squeeze an extra-large measure of butter to fill it out, and to get rid of a little bit of extra weight before tomorrow's first climb. I checked the guide after my recon and it looks like at least a 500 foot climb up to Fairview.

When the noodles are ready I stir the whole sludge together and use my book as a hot pad for the pot. With the pot balanced on my knees, I eat with my right hand and keep my gloved left hand pressed against it for warmth.

Full and warm after eating, I clean up and stow everything away for the night. I check the area around the tarp for the smell, and find that is has dissipated. That's good news, so I move my pad and bag under it for the night. I power through some more of the book before, but am too drowsy to make it through a rather dramatic part. I turn off the light and go to sleep.

Perhaps because of the unresolved action in the book, I sleep fitfully for the next few hours. Unable to stay asleep, I turn on the light and keep reading until the tension is resolved and I feel tired enough to go back to sleep. Already I can see wispy crystals of frost forming on the ground, so I burrow deep in my down bag and sleep till dawn.

9

Despite bundling up, my feet get chilled during the night. Next time I'll try double socks. When it's finally time to get up and moving, I look around in the soft light, preparing for the cold. A light rime coats the underside of my tarp and my breath makes a thick cloud every time I exhale. It takes me a few minutes to get enough momentum to dress and emerge from my bag.

It is certainly the coldest camp since Boomer Branch, and probably even colder than that. My fingers and feet lose feeling quickly. Stomping around camp doesn't seem to help, and only the mug of tea does anything for my numb hands. The only way to get warm is to start hiking, so I get everything loaded and start the two-mile climb up to Fairview and the crossing of Highway 7.

Until I reach the top, I'll be in shade of the ridge I'm ascending, so it's up to me to hike hard enough to return feeling to my extremities. I look around at the sunlight on other ridges and hope for another warm day. The hiking is steep.

It's mornings like these, with frigid temps and tough terrain that make me wonder why I do this. There isn't much pleasure at all in this kind of suffering. And as I continue on, so does the questioning. Why am I doing this for days on end? Is this supposed to be a brief sojourn for self-discovery? I don't feel that it is. In fact, I feel much the same as when I took those first steps 123 miles back.

There is something to be said, though, for being self-reliant in the woods, covering new ground each day, seeing new scenery, and getting all the benefits of fresh air and exercise. And something tangible to look back on: all those mile-posts along the trail.

Also, being away from those teevees, telephones, and traffic—the great noisemakers of our lives—lets the mind wander like a river undammed. I don't see wilderness as a tonic for the hectic lives we lead, but rather as a place for the mind and body to return to normal. Putting one foot in front of the other, day after day, becomes as natural as breathing.

      Each day I'm a bit more eager to see someone else on the trail. But, as of now it's been 48 hours since I've talked with anyone, and I don't anticipate much traffic in the next twenty-mile section of trail. In fact, with a mudslide limiting access further up the trail, I can imagine not seeing anyone else for the rest of the trip. But as long as I don't get hurt, that won't be a problem.

After a long pull up the hill, I am feeling warm and enjoying a flat section of trail. Though the elevation profile of this section shows one long uphill, it's a mix of up and flat. It doesn't seem especially hard, but it is long. The worst part, though, isn't the hiking.

      I'd seen it yesterday as I worked my way over to Buck Branch, and now I'm in it: a sizeable logging cut on the north side of the trail. It is not a scene of total devastation, but close to it. There are some trees left along the trail, as well as some smaller ones inside the unit, but there is logging debris everywhere. There's no way wildlife or humans could make their way through it.

To mark the border of the trail and the unit, there are ribbons of orange flagging hanging at intervals from branches of live trees. I take sections from a few of the ribbons and tie them to my shoulder straps for visibility. Not as good as a vest, but better than nothing.

Without any tree cover, the cold wind pierces through my clothing. I put on my beanie and gloves as I near the top, where the wind is even stronger and colder. The one upside is that the view is more open, allowing me to see much of the wilderness I passed through. Nary a building is visible, just the mountains and the trees.

I know I'm getting close to Fairview when I can hear the rumble of traffic on Highway 7. I'm hoping to find a sheltered spot in the sun to take a snack break. Even though I'm hiking, I'm shivering and ready to get out of the wind.

Up on top is Fairview campground, which I reach after one last grunt from the logging cut. It took me fifty minutes of hiking to get here, though it felt like much longer. I take another look back to the west, towards the ridges and valleys that I've passed over and through—a scene disturbed only by the wasteland below me. It occurs to me that this scar on the landscape is no different than seeing a homeless person on a city street or a starving child on teevee: it doesn't fit into the natural order of things. But it is something very real that needs to be seen, because it gives you something to fight for.

The wind is bitter up here, so I don't linger. I empty the bits of trash from the last three days into a can in the campground, then push on. The campground is, of course, empty. I would not want to camp here in this cold wind. To my surprise, one of the water spigots works, so I top off my bottle. I sign a card at the register and look for other hikers without result. I hoist my pack and walk across the wide, silent highway.

    The sun is out, but not high enough in the sky to warm the air. Once I'm across the road the trees dampen the wind, which helps. I recall mild terrain ahead, and hope the sun stays out. I wish I knew what the weather forecast was, but without a way of knowing I don't have to worry about it.

    Soon the trails skirts another logging cut, deep furrows marking where the skidders dragged up the fallen oaks. The trail is in poor shape here, with deadfall all over. It's not from the logging, just what happens in these woods when the trail isn't maintained. I kick as many branches away as I can , but there are still plenty of fallen trees to go over and around. With the highway not far and a county road just ahead, I think I might come back here with my chainsaw and do some clearing. This is the worst shape the trail has been in since White Rock, 100 miles ago.

At the next stream I drain my water bottle and fill it from the creek. I cross a wide clearing created by logging, which looks like it might have been burned in recent years. The grass has really grown up in the place of the woody mess I saw when I was here two years ago. It looks like a pasture now, easier on the eyes. I bet the deer love it. As I walk on, the dew on the grass gives the air a slightly sweet smell.

After crossing the county road the trail heads uphill for a short ways. Coming over a small I rise, I see a hunter ahead walking slowly and softly, scanning the woods. I make sure to make just enough noise to let him know that it's a human approaching, and he turns slowly towards me as I come up to him.

He asks if I've seen anything, which I haven't, and I ask him if he's had any luck this season, which he hasn't. He shrugs unconcernedly, and we talk for a few moments before he sends me off with a friendly goodbye. I wish him luck as he turns back the way he came.

Off all the hunters I've talked to, none of them have asked about my hike—only if I've seen any deer. If any hunters around here asked me where I started, I'm not sure they'd believe me. But I don't care as long as they don't shoot me.

A few minutes later I scare up two does about 50 yards off the trail. Too bad for the hunter. He'll never know, though.

And the miles roll away as I work my way through the roller-coaster of the trail, up and over to Greenhaw Hollow, then up and over to another Unnamed Creek, and then up the gentle rise of Greenhaw Mountain. I stop briefly in Greenhaw Hollow to admire the cedars clustered in the bottom, blocking out the sun, then continue on.

Despite the ups and downs, it's not as strenuous as other parts of the trail. The climbs and descents are shorter and less steep, allowing me to make good time. The sunshine and lack of wind also help.

After I pass milepost 133 I finally get a good look at the

valley in which I'm hiking. The trail has been running parallel to Richland Creek, a sizeable tributary to the Buffalo River and the namesake of a wilderness area ahead. For about forty miles the trail either parallels Richland Creek or follows one of its tributaries.

But unlike the Hurricane, the trail does not pass through the wilderness, as it was designated so before the construction of the trail. I've day-hiked in the Richland Creek Wilderness a couple of times, and can say that it is a rugged, beautiful place. I feel nearly as strong about it as I do the Hurricane. Both have big valleys and boulder-choked streams; one of the streams in the Richland Creek Wilderness has a gorgeous double waterfall. It's a shame that the trail has to bypass it.

After taking in the vista of the Upper Richland Valley, I follow the trail down towards the crossing of the Richland Creek. My stomach is constantly growling, so I want to find a nice spot for lunch. Before the creek the trail passes through an old abandoned CCC camp from the 1930s. Some of the concrete foundations are still visible, including one building that still has a covered basement. I take a look inside, seeing the usual graffiti and trash (there's a county road nearby, so access is fairly easy).

In contrast, the creek is beautiful: a wide, gentle green stream flowing down from the hills. I'm able to get across on some old washed-up logs that span most of the creek, and once on the other side I find a nice place to sit in the sun. It's turning out to be another terrific day. No issues with feet, knees, or any other part of the body. I pull out my lunch and turn my sweaty back to dry in the sun. Lunch is cheese and tortillas.

Overall, my food planning has gone well. I haven't run out of any of the necessities, only the delicacies. Though the trail mix is bulky, it is still delicious. The suppers have been especially nourishing, since I haven't gone to bed hungry yet. Besides a few minor episodes, I haven't felt especially weak or run down, a sure sign of malnourishment. The vitamins, food, and Emergen-C are doing their work, though I do have to cinch my pants tighter every couple of days. If I run out of food my last day out, I'll consider it perfect.

After the main course, I finish off one of the delicacies: the fig newtons. They don't taste good stale, and they're too dense and heavy to be carried long distances, so I make short work of them. It looks like have a good hill ahead of me, so I need the energy.

Before setting off, I check the guidebook for the terrain ahead and to see where there might be some good areas to camp. I note with satisfaction that I've made over eleven miles by noon today, and that there might be a potential camp spot just a mile and a half ahead. I'm feeling strong still, so I want to see it before calling it a day. It would be nice to find a sunny spot where I can dry out my sleeping bag and tarp from the frosty night before.

I follow the trail up a small side drainage into the cool shade before picking up an old road that leads steeply up the hill. It's a grunt, especially with a full belly, but it's soon over and the grade eases. Walking along in a post-lunch haze, I'm startled by a noisy white truck passing by on a road fifty yards away. There's a small parking lot and trailhead here for access into the Richland Creek Wilderness. In the trail register I'm glad to see that a troop of Boy Scouts has been here recently, using the trail as part of a loop through the wilderness northeast of here. But they're the most recent ones—all the other cards, except for Lucas's, have been nibbled by mice.

After crossing the dirt road I pass through a small

stand of sun-warmed pines, the sharp smell hanging heavily in the air. The trail drops a little bit into a large but shallow bowl, and I start looking for a place to camp. There's a streambed here that is dry by the trail, but is running further downstream. That's a good start. The area is also wide open enough to have sunshine for most of the day, instead of being in a deep valley like last night's camp.

But I still don't see any flat ground to sleep on. I drop my pack so I can recon more quickly, and head down the trail. The only prospective places I see look like they'll require a lot of rock-moving and removing some saplings. Surely I can find a better spot, so I go back to get my pack.

Off the trail about twenty feet there's an old trash dump that I hadn't noticed before. I drop my pack again and spend a few minutes checking it out. There are a lot of glass bottles that look fairly recent, though none have labels. Among the junk is an old bike frame, a crushed metal jerrycan, part of a kids' wagon, and some saw blades—all of it rusty as hell. Also, there's an alarming number of empty oil bottles and old oil filters, all just a few yards from the creek.

Looking around some more, I notice a house in the distance, the green metal roof reflecting the afternoon sunlight. Far too close for comfort for me. That and the trash put me in a bad mood, so I grab my pack and trudge down the trail without looking back.

From my last time here I remember a stand of eastern red cedars somewhere up ahead, as well as a stand of pine beyond it. How far, though, I can't remember. Fortunately, it's only a quarter to two, so I have at least four more hours of light to find a place for the night.

Despite the undemanding hiking and sunshine, the dour mood lasts. Nothing seems to shake it, either. No other camping prospects are appearing, and the only water source I come across is a wildlife pond.

After tramping on for a while, I reach a small stream in the Falling Water Creek drainage. I look around for a flat place nearby, seeing a possibility just upstream. I'm still close to the ridgetop, which is preferable, but when I get to the flat spot I see a four-wheeler trail running nearby. Too close, got to keep going.

Following the stream down, I can see the valley of Falling Water Creek opening up ahead, and it is impressive.

Since Richland Creek there hasn't been much scenery to enjoy, just the woods, so I'm glad for the change.

Finally I reach the stand of pines that I remembered, but there is no flat ground to be seen. From here, the trail dives down through a rocky bluffline, but I stay high to scout for a spot. There isn't much brush to obscure the amazing view, which would make for an amazing campsite, but there's just not a good place.

Bummed that I struck out again, I head on, descending into a rough, rocky ravine. With more light, this area would be a good place to spend some time exploring, but with the afternoon passing quickly, I need to keep going. I find some running water to top off my bottle, barely stopping to fill it and drop the iodine.

I hear a vehicle on the road below before I can see it. But it doesn't take long to get there and my search for a campsite continues. A site here, near the creek, would be convenient, but I don't see any possibilities. Frustrated by the lack of luck, I keep moving. I'll take the next decent site I see.

There's a concrete bridge over Falling Water Creek here, so I take my time as I pass over it, trying to enjoy the beauty of the creek and the view of the valley. I take a few moments to watch the shallow water run over the gray slabs of rock, then continue on.

After the bridge the trail soon leaves the road for the woods. Here I am pleased to see a side road leading to an open campsite just off the trail. I don't like to camp near roads, but seeing as how this one is a dead-end due to a mudslide, I doubt anyone will be using it. Hikers might, though.

There's a nice grove of cedars to put up my tarp in, and a fire ring and wood are in the middle of the small open area. The sun is still shining down here, but not for long. Sunset, though, isn't for several more hours. The air is still comfortable in short sleeves.

After the tarp is up I go down to Falling Water Creek to fetch some water. As I pump the creek water into my bottles, the last of the sunlight leaves the creek bed, replaced by shadow. The ambient light makes the forest glow all around me, so I lounge on a flat rock and enjoy the sight. My pissy mood from earlier is all gone now.

As I gaze over the water and into the wilderness, I hear a slow rumble in the distance. To my surprise, it sounds like a vehicle coming from the closed road, towards the supposed mudslide. I sit and watch as a shiny white suburban and two blue minivans pass, with what look to be government plates. I can't see any faces in the windows, and none of them acknowledge my presence just twenty yards away. I hope they're the only vehicles that pass by.

With my bed and kitchen set up, I have plenty of free time this afternoon. It's still a while before teatime, so I take my pad out into the clearing and stretch out to read. The golden sunlight is shining here in camp.

Reviewing the day's events, I covered much more ground that I thought I would: 16.7 miles. It seems like a lot after the past two short days, and leaves only forty miles till the end of the trail. I have plenty of food to get there, so there's no hurry.

While I pore over my guide and mileage log I hear some voices from near the trail. With my boots off and feet comfortable I don't get up to look, but it sounds like they are coming closer. I don't see anyone and wonder if it is my mind playing tricks on me, now that my mind is unoccupied. I can see most of where the trail passes, but no people appear. Soon the voices are gone again, leaving me mystified. Still only one other hiker seen on the trail.

Before seeing this site, the thought had occurred to me to push on to the Richland Creek Campground and make it another twenty-mile day. But the thought of trying to find my way around an old mudslide in the last light of day did not seem to be a good idea. Anyway, I'd prefer not to camp in any official campgrounds—it's not my style. I doubt the one at Richland Creek is barely used, if at all, because of the road closure to it.

Tea time starts just after the sun sets on camp, about three forty-five. The air is still pleasant, and I enjoy lounging in a t-shirt for a while longer. Once the tea's ready, I take it and my windbreaker over to the creek for a few minutes of meditation. As I cross the road I also enter the wilderness. In an area of such beauty, the official designation seems rather arbitrary.

But then again, most of the things we humans do is arbitrary. Taking a 180-mile walk, for instance. But I do feel peaceful sitting here, watching the water rush down Falling Water Creek.

I leave the wilderness and the creek and return to my

daybed by the fire ring. I have a snack and pick up reading again. After a few pages I can feel goosebumps rising on my arms, so I put on another layer. Thus warmed, I feel drowsy as I try to read and finally put the book aside and put my head down.

When I wake up about twenty minutes later, I feel re-energized. Except when I've missed a night's sleep, I've never been able to nap for more than twenty minutes. It started when I was in my teens and has stayed with me ever since.

I lift my head and look around, wondering if the voices I heard earlier have materialized. They haven't. I pull on my boots and go for a short stroll to loosen up my legs. Though they feel fine, my feet took another beating today. They don't hurt as much as before the last two days, but I think double socks are in order for tomorrow. New insoles, too, are high on the list for when I finish.

In the two hours before supper I manage to plow through a good bit more of *The Brothers Karamazov*, getting a feel for just how much Dostoyevsky was obsessed with morality. But he sure writes a good story. I can't imagine trying to write a story that long and keep it interesting, but nearly 600 pages in I'm still hooked. Few writers can do that well.

The only time I break from reading is to put on more clothing. The damp, cold air is settling down into the drainage, but so far it lacks the bite of last night's cold. I debate starting a fire, but hold off, preferring to cook supper instead.

Reaching blindly into my cook bag for an evening meal, I'm delighted to see that I'll be having shells and cheese. I need a break from regular noodles, though I'm hungry enough for it not to matter much. Just something hot and filling is what I'm craving. I think I'll save the other mac and cheese for the last night, though.

While I'm gathering up the ingredients, I see a bright light appear in the sky, above the ridge to the west. At first I think it's another of the many small planes that fly over the area, though I don't usually see them this late—it's almost completely dark. As I watch, I notice that whatever it is, it doesn't have running lights. It doesn't seem to be a satellite, either, because it doesn't dim as it moves across the sky. I begin to wonder what the hell it really is.

I don't see a contrail, like a high-flying airliner would

leave behind, though it does seem to have forward facing lights. This is getting weird.

It passes directly overhead, but there is no sound, as surely there would be from a plane or helicopter. I think of the Air Force Base a hundred miles to the south and wonder if it has anything to do with it. The object soon clears the ridge to the east, leaving me mystified. I occasionally look up from cooking to see if it returns, but it doesn't. I have no idea what it was.

As for my supper, the shells and cheese are delicious, but heavy. My appetite is stronger than ever, but it still takes me forty-five minutes to consume my two-plus pounds of noodles.

Following custom, I wash the pot and put my things away, then consult the guide to plan for tomorrow. From here, the trail turns north till it reaches the Buffalo River. Though that is the proper end to the OHT, I will take a right and follow the Buffalo River Trail (BRT) all the way to its end, another fifteen miles.

Though I've floated many sections of the Buffalo River and hiked part of the BRT upstream, this will be the first time I've set foot on this section. I'm looking forward to it.

But before I get there, I have a lot country to hike through. The scenery is incredible for much of the way, with big water and big hills all around. As far as I can tell, there's only one more significant climb for the rest of the hike, which I'll reach tomorrow. If the weather continues to be good, the views will be amazing up towards the Buffalo River Valley, home to one of the last free-flowing rivers in this part of the world.

After coming up with a plan for tomorrow, I decide it's time to head to bed and hunker down before I sleep. I take my pad back over to the tarp and get out my sleeping bag to use as a blanket. I read for a while more, but the fatigue from the day sets in, and I don't fight it.

As I lay there, drifting off to sleep, I realize that I don't have long to go. Only two more nights and forty more miles to go. Out here, the end of the trail seems abstract. I hope the woods go on forever.

10

I sleep through the night undisturbed. No other strange lights appeared overhead, and it didn't feel as cold as the previous night. Looking around in the faint light, I see no frost. A glance up at the clear pre-dawn sky bodes well for the day, also.

Camp is packed up and I'm on the trail just after seven. Because I'm on the west side of the ridge, it'll be a while before I see the sun. The trail parallels Falling Water Creek for the next four miles, as well as a road below. A short climb right off the bat gets the blood pumping, and despite a bit of stiffness in the legs I feel good and strong this morning.

Somewhere up ahead is the purported mudslide, and

I'm getting more and more curious as to what kind of shape the trail is in. If it was big enough to shut down a forest road, it must be sizeable. Though I'm not sure exactly where it is, I am sure I will see it in the next two hours. I wonder how much I'll have to detour around it. This day could get very interesting.

Through the trees I get an occasional glimpse of the creek below, though not nearly as many as I would like. It sounds wild down there.

Glancing upwards, I see a few wayward clouds speeding across the morning sky, an ominous sign. The winds are picking up on the ridges, so a storm might be blowing in. I just hope I have a few hours of sunshine. For now, though, the air is tranquil and I plod along steadily.

After passing mile marker 142 I see a line of upturned earth directly ahead. As I draw near it looks rather innocuous: it's a mudslide all right, but only about 75 yards long and about 5-10 feet wide. Hardly the swath of devastation I'd imagined. There's an easy and obvious route going uphill and to the left, so I climb up a small drop and hike on the level to pass around it. I start to wonder if the stories I heard were really true, or just exaggerated. Luke said there was flagging around it, but I see none here. Nor does the slide go all the way to the road—it is still hung up above it here. I step back down to the official trail, where a white blaze on a tree is a welcome sight. I shrug my shoulders and keep going, glad not to be delayed.

Five or ten minutes later, I'm not sure, I come to another small drainage from which I can see a large exposed section of light brown earth: the real thing. The whole hillside has been washed away down to the road. It looks like a large hydraulic mining operation. Trees are down, boulders from the cliffs above are scattered all over, and dried mud is all that remains. I want to take a closer look.

Rather than go above or below the slide, I start looking for a way across. It looks daunting and a bit dangerous; perhaps the road below might be a better option, though it, too, sustained quite a bit of damage.

Lucas was right, though, someone did flag a route across this mess. I see a small sprig of pink flagging just uphill, so I start to follow it. Every step I take feels like I'm walking on eggshells. Knowing that the most unstable part of the ground is gone doesn't quell all the doubts in my mind. I look up at the rocky bluffline above and hope that it doesn't decide to cut loose while I'm here. Further ahead I can see where the flag line leads, which looks to be the most direct way across. A few faint bootprints mark the way, in addition to the flagging.

Once I'm across and back on trail, I take a few minutes to survey the damage. The newly exposed rock on the bluffline stands in stark contrast to the dark, weathered rocks that have fallen down into the scar beside me. I imagine that this section of rock might have set off the whole slide when it cut loose and hit the steep, supersaturated ground below it. What a sight it must've been when that happened. I would love to have seen it.

After a few pictures I continue on, noting that the sky is darkening with clouds. I can now hear the wind in the top of the trees; they sway with every gust. It isn't long before the wind penetrates to the ground, so I zip up my windbreaker and bitch to myself. I really don't want another windy, cold morning or more rain.

But as I continue hiking, the wind keeps increasing, probably due to the confluence of the Falling Water Creek and Richland Creek Valleys just ahead. I don't want to stop, but I need more water. In the time it takes to pull out my water bottle and dip it in the creek, my hand gets ice cold, almost numb. I quickly throw in the iodine tabs and start jogging to warm up.

There's nothing to block the wind when I cross the bridge over Richland Creek, though I still stop for a picture of the beautiful, though uninviting, green creek. Once over the bridge I follow the trail as it takes a right back into the woods, where I'm more sheltered from the wind, but not as much as I'd like to be.

When I sign in at the trail register, I don't even bother checking for other hikers. No cars can reach here, and it's not the weekend, when most hikers would venture out here. I need to keep moving to stay warm.

It was somewhere around here that Lucas turned around on his hike, probably at the campground. I wonder what he felt, having walked all this way and then retracing his steps. Was he excited, or did he dread walking over the same ground? Technically, the scenery is the same, but different times of day and conditions certainly make it look different. And he knew where he could get water and where good places to camp were. He sure seemed to be enjoying himself when I saw him eleven days and 130 miles ago.

I wish I could say the same for myself right now, trudging along in the frigid wind. Though rocky, the terrain here is gentle. A snack break would be good for me, but not in these conditions. Watching more clouds roll overhead, I wonder about getting out my rain gear for the deluge I fear is coming. If there's a sheltered spot up ahead I'll do it.

Despite the miserable conditions, the view down onto Richland Creek is gorgeous. Though the wilderness is behind and to the west of us, this is still rugged country. I try to imagine what this area looked like before it was logged. Judging from stumps three and four feet in diameter, it must've been quite a sight.

About a mile after leaving the road the trail steers away from the creek and into a series of small hollows that cut into the ridge to the west. Though I can't see the top of it, I can roughly gauge the height from the ridge opposite me, and it looks imposing. But the trail keeps climbing steadily, leaving my legs and lungs none the worse for wear.

Though the hollows are each wonderful, the multitude of rocks is working my ankles over. Though I want to look around at the forest through which I'm passing, I have to concentrate on the trail immediately before to prevent rolling my ankles. At least the wind isn't as strong here.

Out of the corner of my eye I spy a patch of blue to the southeast and watch it till it closes back into the folds of gray. I hope it is a sign that the front passing through will be a dry one.

If it stays cold and windy I plan to push hard, getting as far as possible even if it's raining. The end is now 35 miles away, doable in two long days. The thought of spending a night by a warm fire in a warm bed is incredibly appealing at this point.

As the next miles pass I see the clouds are breaking up, though the wind does not relent. The sun is breaking through in places, and the little bits that reach me feel delightful. In fact, by the time I reach mile 148 the sky has cleared. I celebrate by taking a break in Armstrong Hollow, the finest hollow I've seen today. The improving weather helps.

The boulders here are immense, and I can only imagine what it looks like further up- and downstream of here. During the wet time of year, this whole area would be full of waterfalls. And I don't think it would be miserable to be here during a spring rain, when the temps are warm enough. Even if it weren't warm, the beauty would be everywhere.

With this improvement in the weather, I don't feel as rushed. It might very well turn out to be a warm and pleasant day. I alter my plans, aiming for a campsite about four miles away, near mile 152. The guide makes it sound like a perfect place: it's near a waterfall and an old homestead. Surely there will be flat ground there.

The sun is now on my back, so I set off, grateful for the good weather. From here the trail climbs for the next three miles—the last major climb, as far as I can tell. From there it goes over the ridge, and on the way down is the prospective campsite. If I keep a good pace I can reach it by lunchtime.

The only break I take for the next hour is to take off my windbreaker. Though still windy, the sun is warm enough to override it. Before putting my pack back on, I take some time to enjoy the spectacular view to the south, including the Richland Creek Wilderness. Wild country.

I know I'm getting close to the top as the trail levels off. Though my stomach is growling, I feel great, drinking in the scenery and genuinely enjoying myself. It's a great day to be alive and on the trail.

As I cross the forest road on top, I see a school bus several hundred feet down the road. At first I think it's just a bus driver taking a break on a rural road, then it occurs to me just how far out this is. Getting closer, I see that the door is open and an old metal drum sits nearby. There are no footprints in the ground, and no other signs of life are visible, so it must be abandoned. But why all the way out here? Strange.

A bit later I cross another forest road and pass by a trailhead parking area. This is the Stack Rock Trailhead, though Stack Rock itself is somewhere off the trail to the north. I walk through the empty parking area, following an old road to a gate. A sign on the gate cheers me: *Foot Travel Invited*. I like that very much, much better than "No Bikes" or "No Vehicles". I feel welcomed just walking past the gate, as if Old Smokey the Bear himself were here to greet me as I reenter the woods.

As I start down into the next drainage, I can once again feel the wind penetrating through the trees. And it's cold, moreso now that I'm leaving the sunlight for shade as the trails drops onto a more northerly aspect.

The potential campsite lies just ahead, and I look forward to seeing it. I don't remember the homestead at all from my previous hike here. After crossing a small stream, the trail reaches a point on the bluffline. This is the site. There's a good overlook of the Dry Creek drainage, below and to the north. Across the drainage from me is an impressively long bluffline. All the rocks and nooks make for good bear habitat, particularly with the southern exposure.

Unfortunately the wind is gusting strongly here, chilling me to the bone such that I have to step behind a tree to shelter myself as a put on my windbreaker. The cold sweat where my pack sat on my back feels like it's turning to ice in the few seconds I'm stooping over, tussling with my jacket and pack straps. Nearby I see the remains of the homesteader's cabin, with only the chimney left for posterity.

There are several choice sites for camping here, and the nearby stream will be good for water. But after considering it for a few moments, I think the wind would be just too cold and strong for this to be a comfortable place to spend the night. Even the five minutes I take to eat lunch are miserable, so I pack up and keep going, making a mental note to come back when the weather is more mild.

Fortunately, I know of another campsite about a mile ahead further down into Dry Creek. To regain some warmth, I jog along the level trail till I'm on a more sheltered stretch of trail. Looking up, I notice that the trees on this side of the ridge have more of their leaves than the other side. It isn't as open here, which helps cut the wind. But I like the way the leaves filter and scatter the autumn light on the forest floor here, though I keep moving to stay warm.

Close to the bottom of the drainage, I recognize the area: I've camped here before. I stop and look around for a place to put the tarp, occasionally looking up to see what the weather's doing. The wind isn't too bad down here, though I can hear it howling down the flanks of Horn Mountain to the west. With that in mind, I pitch my tarp tightly, with the foot end into the wind and steeply tilted towards the ground. That should block most of the wind, especially if I put my pack at my feet when I go to bed.

After the tarp is up, I sit in the sun for a few minutes, near the fire ring. But it doesn't take long for me to get chilled again, so I crawl under my tarp and pull out the sleeping bag for warmth. It's early afternoon and I'm wearing nearly every article of clothing I brought. It'll be a bitter night.

I can only read for twenty minutes before I get antsy. Despite my best efforts, the wind is still noisily whipping the tarp, driving me crazy. I decide it'd be a good time to fill up on water, so I grab the bottles, pot, and filter and walk down to Dry Creek. I'm thankful that the narrow creek bed is sheltered, and I linger for a few sunny minutes after everything is topped off.

Back in camp, I start thinking about building a fire. There's a fire ring here, but almost no firewood in the immediate area—it's been picked clean. Being the most commonly used site in this area, I'm not surprised. But with the wind so gusty, I decide against a fire and instead start looking for a more sheltered place to sleep.

Uphill there's a level bench of ground, on which runs a four-wheeler trail. I scout it anyway, noting that the wind seems less persistent up here. I see a few options, but nothing that great. I think I'll stay parked where I am for now.

When I return to my things, I put on my rain jacket and another pair of socks. Now I have everything on. Though it's lightweight, the rain jacket has become a great layering piece for cold, windy days. I cinch the hood down over my beanie, which helps hold in the heat even better.

As the afternoon wears on, the wind wears on my nerves. At times it blows so hard that it presses the tarp into my lower body. The gusts have to be fifteen to twenty miles an hour.

When it's time for tea, I waste no time out in the open and return to the warm cocoon of my sleeping bag with all possible speed. Looking up, I see some strato-cumulus clouds sailing overhead. Not a good sign. I might be in for some precipitation after all.

After a few sips of the exceptionally strong tea, my patience with the wind finally wears out. I head back uphill to the four-wheeler trail and scout one of the flat places. After moving some rocks and figuring out where to guy the tarp, I start moving camp up there. The wind thrashes the tarp as I untie the lines from the anchor trees, and by the time I start to string it up again, the lines have worked themselves into a formidable series of Gordian knots.

As I work them loose and re-pitch the tarp, the wind picks up again and I have a hell of time getting it set up. Perhaps I was wrong about the wind being calmer up here. Feeling the surge of frustration with the wind, along with a burst of energy from the caffeine, I throw a tantrum. Cursing the wind, I throw sticks, leaves, stones, and old empty beer cans until I get it all out of my system.

The forest around me seems exceptionally quiet now. The brief meltdown has warmed me up considerably, and I calmly finish setting up my new camp before settling in to read for the afternoon.

As I relax, I notice the wind keeps switching around: from south to west and back and forth and in between. It is relentless. I don't feel like moving again, so I finish my tea and continue reading. There's nothing I can do about it anyway. I pass the next few hours immersed in my book

Long after the sunshine is gone from camp, the reflected sunlight is spectacular in the western sky: deep oranges and reds slowly fade to gray, like a great forest fire burning out. As if in its own wild celebration, the wind continues whipping through the trees, bending some of the nearby ones at unsafe angles. In addition to the cold, now I have falling trees to worry about.

For my next-to-last supper, I get the creamy chicken-flavored noodles. I add extra milk powder to fatten it up and get rid of the weight. With only two more days to go, there's no need to ration it. I huddle over the stove with my back to the wind, now blowing downhill and down drainage.

Eating improves my mood considerably and stokes my internal fire. Some chili powder or hot sauce would be ideal for times like tonight—I make a note to include that the next time I'm out in the cold.

Overhead, the icy white stars are shining through the cold night air. No clouds are building. I can see the glow from electric lights from over the ridge to the northwest, though cannot for the life of me figure out what town it could be. I check the trail guide map to see if I can figure it out, but it's too small to include much of the surrounding area. I also keep an eye out for any strange lights in the sky, but there are none to be seen this evening.

After I close up the kitchen and put the food away, I go back to bed to plan for tomorrow and read until either sleep or the cold drives me into my bag.

In my guide, the elevation profile for tomorrow looks mellow. Really mellow. That means I should be able to make good time between here and the Buffalo River, about eleven miles away. With the cold temperature and a shady first few miles, I plan to forgo breakfast and hoof it until I reach a sunny spot where I can take a leisurely morning tea and meal. With all the creeks and hollows ahead, I'm sure I'll have no trouble finding a good place. I put some powdered tea in my water bottle for an early-morning lift for the first few miles. I just hope it doesn't freeze.

As the evening passes, the wind finally mellows, having blown for at least eight straight hours here. I used to think that the canyons of southern Utah were bad for wind, but today has taught me otherwise.

Like the wind, I've expended nearly all my energy, too. By ten I put *The Brothers Karamazov* to bed and gather the last few thoughts to ramble into my tape recorder. I recall spending the night in this same area many years ago on a similarly frigid night. So cold was it then, that I had to fill a bottle with hot water to keep in my sleeping bag to keep my feet from freezing. It was a miserable night, one of the coldest I've ever spent in the woods. I'm glad I have a much warmer sleeping bag now.

Burrowing deep into my bag to sleep, I picture my girlfriend snuggled up in a warm bed two thousand miles away, while I lay on the ground in the dirt with frost already forming around me.

11

Though it's barely light when my alarm goes off the next morning, I don't bother with my headlamp and instead go straight to work. It's as cold as I figured it'd be: positively wintry. But my determination seems to be working harder than any other part of my brain, so I have everything packed away and ready to go before the sky is even fully lit.

The rocky trail down to the creek jars my sleepy, cold bones. I manage to avoid slipping on the icy rocks in the creek, though a steep, slick step on the other side nearly puts me on the ground. I catch myself and begin a short climb up the north side of Dry Creek.

After several minutes of hiking, I glance at my watch and am pleased to see that it's only a quarter to seven. That's half an hour before my usual getaway time. Though I'm still hiking in shadow, I'm already warm. I'm reluctant to stop until I'm in the sunlight, so during the flat stretches I take out the bag of mini-wheats from my leg pocket to get something in my belly. I don't want to ruin an early start by crapping out latter from a lack of energy. The tea in my water bottle is partially frozen, though a few vigorous shakes breaks enough loose to drink.

Richland Creek flows somewhere off to my right, and all the little hollows through which I'm hiking flow into it. Up to my left is Horn Mountain, one of the last of the mountains on this part of the Ozark Plateau. The terrain to the east of here is not nearly so rugged as what I've passed through. The hardest part of the hike is behind me.

In less than an hour I reach the boundary of the Ozark National Forest. For the first time in over 150 miles I'm back on state land, though there's no discernible difference to my eyes.

But the best part is that the sun is finally topping the

ridge to the east and can begin burning off the frost. It is a wonderful feeling, indeed, to be walking into the sunlight on a frosty morning with no clouds in the sky. It's another great way to start the day. I eat another bite of cereal and take a swallow of tea and keep moving.

Above me is the long bluffline I could see from the old homestead yesterday. After a few more miles I should be out of the mountains and in the more pastoral part of the valley, closer to the Buffalo. I know there's a long road walk ahead, so I enjoy being in the woods for this last bit.

The mild terrain and warming temperatures make for pleasurable walking. A glance at my watch shows that I'm making three miles an hour, even with breaks. The sun is rising higher in the morning sky and frost blooms litter the barren forest floor. Rocks still sprawl over the trail, but I don't mind them. The lichen and moss that grows on the occasional cluster of boulders is beautiful.

Even though this area is for game management, I haven't seen either game or hunters. The strips of flagging still hang on the front of my pack, and though it's bright enough now to clearly be seen, I did feel somewhat uneasy earlier in the day about being mistaken for an animal.

Down valley I hear the high whine of a machine, but cannot tell if it's heading this way. It's been since day before yesterday since I heard any rifle fire.

Searching my memory, I can't recall if the Park Service allows hunting on Buffalo National River land or not, though I'm thinking it does. Either way, I will keep the flagging on as insurance for any itchy trigger fingers out here.

When I reach an old road, I figure I have five or six miles to go till I reach the river, and it's all road from here. The Richland Valley is just ahead, as well as the boundary of the Buffalo National River. When I reach the boundary, I stop and take a sit-down break. A waist-high lichen covered rock off to the side provides a perfect perch for a few minutes of rest and snacking. It is now warm enough for me to take off my long underwear leggings, which I do using the rock as support. Nonetheless, I still stumble as I free my right foot, and nearly end up on the ground in my boxers. I laugh at myself and put my pants back on while I take a few more minutes to rest.

My desire to get to the river is quickly mounting, so I soon take off on the roadwalk. I follow it down a small hill, where it runs along the west side of the Richland Creek

Valley. This marks the transition of the surroundings from sylvan to pastoral, though it is still beautiful. The pastures are wide and green, set off by barbed wire and old fence posts. There are no more blazes to follow—a Park Service rule, I believe--but the route is unmistakable.

At a road junction I see an old wooden sign with "Lake Fort Smith 161" and an arrow pointing back the direction I came from. The thrilling realization of just how far I've come really hits home for the first time. Only nineteen miles remain until the finish, but on this gorgeous autumn day I don't ever want it to end.

I've never liked roadwalks. Several years earlier I spent two months in Ecuador, where many of my trips into the backcountry had a considerable amount of them. It was especially miserable when the local *camionetas* would roar by, overloaded with people and spraying dirt and gravel in their wake.

But here it's different, better. You could probably go back in time 50 years and not notice anything different here except newer fence posts. The road is seldom traveled; the tracks on it look a few days old at least. There are a few hardy souls who live out this way, but not many. But on this glorious autumn day, I have this lovely shaded country lane to myself.

In one of the many I fields I pass, there is a grand old oak, one of the biggest I've ever seen. It has a whole pasture to itself, and has grown full and fat in its old age. Branches swoop down and outward from its thick, gray bole, close enough to the ground for even a small child to climb up on it and sit for a spell. I'm a bit surprised it doesn't have a rope swing on it: the setting is perfect for one.

Stopping to admire it, I am reminded of the baobob trees I saw in East Africa the year before, those wise old denizens of the African savanna. Though I saw many of them, I wish I could've touched one, just to feel what something that old and majestic feels like.

Now I'm tempted to jump the fence and see the oak close up, but a distant rumble on the road sounds like a vehicle approaching. I stay on my side of the fence and take some pictures, though the tree is too large and I am too close to fit it into the frame of my camera. So I wave goodbye to the grand old hermit oak and head down the road.

Up around the next bend I see a plume of dust on the

road, getting closer. A few seconds later, a massive truck comes into view. It's an old rusty tow truck, big enough to handle the semis. I quickly scramble up the roadbank on the left to get out of the way. There isn't enough room on the road for both of us, and the truck shows no sign of stopping. As it passes, the red-faced driver and I exchange friendly waves. It's the closest I've come to human contact in more than two days and thirty miles of trail.

As the road makes a wide arc to the left, I can see a bare stretch of bluff to the north. I'm getting close to the river. I tell myself I'll be there in twenty minutes, but manage to make it in fifteen. I've never been good at estimating distances, even in open flat ground. A glance at my watch shows that I've covered the last three miles in forty-five minutes.

The bluff I've reached is a section called The Nars, because it is a long, narrow fin of bluff that separates the verdant fields of Richland Creek Valley from the Buffalo River to the west. I scramble up the short spurt trail and am rewarded by a breathtaking view of the blue-green river. I stash my pack at the top of the trail and hop along the increasingly narrow rock, careful not to snag my feet on the many ridges and holes in the rock.

The wind has died away, leaving only the still air. Below me, the river runs smooth and quiet. Signs of the major flood this past spring are everywhere: upturned trees, heavily-bent willows, and dry detritus hanging astonishingly high in the riverside trees. It must have been an incredible sight to see then. It is a beautiful, peaceful sight this morning.

I cross the foot-wide neck of the bluff to other, higher side. From here I have a lovely view both upstream of the Buffalo and overlooking the Richland Valley. Looking up the latter, I can see the ridge I crossed yesterday, as well as the northern end of Horn Mountain the bluffs under which I hiked earlier this morning. This is wonderfully gentle country I've entered, here near the eastern edge of the Ozark Plateau. Upstream on the Buffalo is higher and more rugged country, spectacular even, but I'm content to sit here for a while and enjoy this scenery. I've hiked a long way to see it.

Before leaving I take a self-portrait with the timer on my camera. I want to get as much of the Nars as possible, along with my pack and myself. It takes some time to figure out how to position it on the uneven rocky surface, but in the end it works. It's crooked, but I like to think it makes it look better. I take one more look at the long horizon, then shoulder my back and climb back down to the road.

Now it's just over a mile to the Buffalo, at a spot called Woolum. That's the official end of the OHT. The closer I get, the more sandy the road becomes, making the walking a bit more taxing. The tall brown grass along the way seems to be alive with little birds, chirping and singing happily in the sun. The air is still and pleasantly warm.

It only seems to take a few minutes, but I reach the river. Though I'll keep going, I am excited to reach this point. I can feel the joy of other hikers who have hiked this far, 165 miles. It's quite a walk.

Because the first six miles of the trail have been closed for a while, I may be the first person to have completed it all in a thru-hike in six and a half years. It's a flattering thought, but it doesn't really matter. Many have hiked it before me, and many will after. The trail doesn't care.

But I'm glad I don't have to cross the river—it looks like a cold adventure. Across the rippling water I see two vehicles parked there: a private car and a government truck. I might see some other hikers, after all.

After a few minutes at Woolum I take a right, downstream, which immediately crosses the last section of Richland Creek before it empties into the Buffalo. Like the river, it is wide and cold here, but only knee-deep. Once on the other side I lounge in the sun while my feet dry. After I filter some water, I celebrate the beautiful day and the arrival at Woolum by having the second milkshake of the trip. The cold water makes it extra-delicious, and I wash out the package several times to get every last bit.

With my feet dry, I put my shoes and boots back on and prepare to continue. It is still well before noon. I consult the guide to look for potential campsites. I've come eleven miles so far today, so I'll be looking for something in the next five or six miles. As long as I can get to a place with some daylight remaining, I'll be happy.

The next fifteen miles, the last of the trip, will be all new to me. I'll be hiking on the south side of the Buffalo, but have to find the trail first. With my boots and pack back on, I set off across the green field to the east, soon finding the narrow, but distinct path that will take me all the way to the end.

Once I'm back in the shade, the temperature drops back down

to cold. Frost blooms dot the sides of the trail and will until the sun reaches them. After all the flat walking this morning, I'm glad the trail gets into some terrain again as it quickly picks its way up the next hill and into the woods. For my efforts I'm rewarded with a pleasant view of the river, and can see the wide green hayfields that make up most of the bottomland here. Even though it's November and the past few nights have been freezing, the grass still glimmers green in the midday sunshine.

    From here the trail heads away from the river and back into the trees. After passing a confusing intersection with a horse trail, the foot trail picks up an old roadbed that likely hasn't been used by vehicles in the more than thirty years this area has been a national park.

    As if to confirm this, I come across the guts of an old car long since abandoned. Why it was abandoned out here I have no idea. The interior is rotted and rusty, and bullet holes pockmark the rear end. The tailfins, though, are still intact.

    Further on I come to the still-standing ruins of an old house. The roof has caved in, but the walls remain upright. I take a look around, careful not to step on any of the rusty nails sticking up out the disintegrating boards on the ground.

There's not much to see, just scattered detritus from both man and mouse. The thought and threat of hantavirus keeps me from getting too curious.

After that stop, the trail continues on the level. It's just after noon and the sun feels wonderful. I pass through a small stand of eastern cedars, thrilled by the fresh and fragrant aroma. Juncos and sparrows flit around me as I pass through, singing their quick and pretty songs.

Soon the old roadbed begins heading towards the river. Rocks and clay make up most of the walking surface, and show no sign of other hikers. Here and there I see a faint horseshoe track mud, but nothing I would consider recent. But this is not exactly an area with easy access: there's the ford at Woolum a couple miles back, or the other end of the trail twelve miles ahead. There are some roads back here, but their rough condition and distance discourage most folks from coming out here for fun.

The river, somewhere ahead, is the easiest way to see this country, and perhaps the best. It's been nearly twenty years since I floated through here, but I remember the experience fondly. I surely wouldn't have guessed then that I would still be exploring this country, finding enough to keep me busy for the rest of my life.

On the way down I think I hear voices in the air, but when I stop to listen I hear only the birds. In my experience, the longer I'm away from other humans, the more other sounds remind me of people. I take a quick look behind, but seeing nothing I continue to the bottom of the descent.

My hearing didn't fool me after all: there I see four figures through the underbrush, each wearing bright orange caps. As they draw closer it's obvious they aren't hunters: they look a bit old to be roaming the woods for game, and instead of rifles, they have binoculars and cameras. Finally, other hikers! I can't help smiling as we meet.

After a quick round of pleasantries, they ask me where I'm coming from. I tell them, then add: "You're the first hikers I've seen in 150 miles," which really surprises them. As they quiz me about my hike, I note the logos on their hats of a popular outing club.

It turns out that they've been section-hiking the OHT by day-hikes for years. One of them volunteers that "It's taken us eleven years to do what you've done in eleven days."

"Well," I reply, "I also took a number of years to section-hike it. The important thing is that you're out here doing it." I truly admire them for being out here, and doubt I could've met a friendlier and more receptive group of fellow hikers.

Just before we head our separate ways I ask them if there's a good spot ahead to have lunch. They excitedly shake their heads yes, with the leader telling me that the trail comes to a nice bluff just a little ways ahead: "a perfect place to sit awhile." One of the other gentlemen adds that they watched a Bald Eagle ride the thermals around the bluff for forty-five minutes.

I thank them and wish them luck as they head up the hill. They're heading for Woolum—it was their car I saw across the river. We wave goodbye and go our own ways, and they are soon out sight and earshot.

A few minutes down the trail I start the climb up to the bluff that they had recommended to me. With a hungry belly nagging me, I begin the grunt up the hill. Less than fifteen minutes later the trail levels off again and through the trees I see only sky. The path splits two ways as I near the bluff, so I take the one that leads to the edge.

I'm rewarded with the best view of the river so far, even better than the one from the Nars. It's a good 75-100 feet down to the river, and across the valley I can see the limestone bluffs that make the river so scenic. Looking downstream I get a close-up view of the aptly named White Bluff, where the trail will soon take me.

But before I continue on, I find a nice shelf of rock jutting over the river that looks like it has the finest view in the area. Sure enough, I sit in the sun while I eat another tortilla and peanut butter lunch, watching the low river slowly flow down its cobbled bed. The hayfields are so bright green that they are hard to look at without sunglasses. My heart sings with joy as the afternoon unfolds its warmth and beauty.

While lounging in the sun, I check the guide for any camping prospects ahead. This spot has convinced me that the bluff-tops are they way to go, so I make a note of the ones ahead and will see what I feel like in the next few miles.

Not till I leave do I realize that the eagle the men had spoken of wasn't there. I look back towards the bluff and the open space beyond, but I don't see it. The memory of the one I saw on my first day out will have to suffice.

By one-thirty I've covered fifteen miles for the day, though that speaks more to the ease of the terrain than to my speed. Soon I'm back on a roadwalk, cruising along a wide field to my left. Nearby is another abandoned car, rusting in the woods. This area has more rusted vehicles than any other Park Service unit I've ever been in.

It takes me a minute, but I figure that these cars might very well have been left here on purpose as a protest against the National Park. To acquire all this land, the government did what it felt it needed to do to obtain the land. I'm sure the residents at the time did not want to give up and their land and go. And though I've never heard anyone in these parts say anything against the Park outright (it's certainly brought a lot of tourism dollars in), I'm sure there's a lot of grumbling among the locals who were here before the Park Service was.

One woman in particular, Granny Henderson, silently embodied the spirit of protest in a very admirable way. When told back in the early 70s that her land would revert to government ownership when she died, she did the most rebellious thing of all by living a long life. She kept animals on her land right up to the end, feeding and taking care of them as well as anyone could.

Her cabin still stands in the Upper Buffalo Valley, miles upstream. An old, yellowing article about her is posted on the porch of her now-vacant cabin. The article contains a picture of a tiny woman of great determination and a hint of sadness in her eyes. She was the last living link in the area to the early settlers, dying in her eighties about twenty years ago. Her old cabin—the last time I saw it—was rotting away and falling apart.

Now that the going is nice and camp not too far away, I find myself in no hurry, sauntering along a seldom-used road. There's plenty of light left in the day, and the thought that I will be done hiking tomorrow weighs heavily on me. What will I do when I don't have miles ahead of me to hike? But before I get too deep into such sentiment, I shift the focus back to now. I soon reach the end of the road and cross a small creek, glad to be back in the trees.

The climb I've been expecting for a while soon rises before me. It will be good to get out of the shade of the small hollow I'm hiking in and back into the afternoon sun. I grunt my way up the hill and in a matter of minutes am once again at a fantastic view of the river. Wild and scenic, indeed.

A bit further along I find a good lookout downstream to Whisenant Bluff, my prospective campsite for tonight. From here it looks like there's a decent bit of flat ground up there, as well as a grove of pine trees near the bluff's edge. But to get up there I've got to go down first.

The next issue will be water: specifically, will there be water in the next creek, Whisenant Hollow? If not, I suppose I can bushwhack down to the river. But the prospect of carrying full water bottles, pot, and mug back up through the underbrush would be tricky. I'd have to make it work.

Fortunately my question is soon answered: there is water in the creek, though not much. I breathe a sigh of relief. Since I'll be boiling the water in the pot and mug, I don't bother filtering it.

With everything topped up, I have the heaviest load in days, probably since I resupplied. The extra weight makes the trail to the top of the bluff seem steep and merciless, but it is also short. Coming over the top I see a few marginal sites, but when I get to the flat top I whoop with joy: plenty of flat ground, logs to sit on, a fire ring with fire wood stacked beside it, and an amazing view overlooking the river valley. I'm so excited to see such a wonderful site that I don't even bother taking off my pack before venturing over to the edge of the bluff. I can't believe my good luck. This place has everything.

The woods around me shine in the afternoon light as I set up camp. The mix of sun, scenery, and luck puts me in a wonderful mood. Plus, there's no wind. I sing as I pitch my tarp and set up the kitchen. Looking at the ample supply of firewood both stacked beside the ring and scattered in the woods around, I know it's going to be a good night. I take my book to the edge of the bluff to read for the rest of the afternoon.

To the northwest I can see a prominent mountain topped with antennae. I figure that Harrison, the closest big town, must be over that way. I can see the same mountain from my parents' place to the west of here. The sight of familiar landmarks always makes me feel better.

Just across the river valley, I can see a very nice house perched on the edge of a bluff, much like the one I am on. The broad, south-facing windows glint in the afternoon sunshine. How lucky they are to have a view like this every day. I've only been here half an hour and it's overwhelming me.

For having covered eighteen and a half miles today I feel surprisingly fresh, no doubt buoyed by the good weather and scenery. There is something about a sunny day that just makes me feel more energetic. Additionally, knowing I only have about seven and a half miles to go tomorrow is exciting, though it goes both ways. I don't have long until I finish, but I'm not sure I want to.

    Instead of reading, I reflect back on the trip. I remember the many worries about my feet, and how they seem so long ago. I recall the long push of the Big Day, which seems ancient history, though it was less than a week ago. When I'm on the trail the days seem long, but when I reach camp they seem like they've flown by. It's a weird dichotomy I've never quite understood. But why do I need to? It's enough just to enjoy it.

My last tea time is celebrated with the strongest cup of tea yet, spiking my energy again. Doing all my camp chores for the last time gives them a sort of novelty, which I relish.

    I really do love being out in the woods. Two of the happiest summers of my life were as a Forest Service hotshot, camping out 100-plus nights a summer. I'm willing to forgo the luxuries—hot showers, comfortable bed, cold beer—for days or weeks on end to get to go places that few have been, and see things few have seen. It's always been worth the discomfort and misery, every damn day of it.

By 1645 the sun has finally set in the west, from my point of view somewhere in the north end of the Richland Creek Wilderness. Flocks of geese fly south overhead, catching the last burning rays of the dying sun on their soft, light bellies. I watch the flocks expand and contract as if held together by a rubber band, until they pass out of sight.

Twilight always seems shortest in the late fall and winter. The longer summer days seem to stretch out at the beginning and the end, as if to celebrate the drama of sunrise and sunset. Not so this time of year. With the darkness and cold coming on quick, I start the fire and break up some of the largest branches for later.

    As soon as the fire's going good I get out the makings for supper: a large last meal of macaroni and cheese. I place the water-filled pot close to the fire to start heating it, though I'm not yet ready to start cooking.

    The light, dry sticks burn quickly, so I make a tepee out of some of the larger ones. To my dismay, the pine isn't taking, so I weed it out of the woodpile and scatter the smaller pieces without leaving the fireside.

Catching a glimpse of the fading western sky, I move my sitting log around to watch the last of the flaming colors of sunset fade away to gray, then black. The setting could not be more perfect. A current of excitement and joy is still running through me, unable to be contained.

Looking across the river valley to the north, I see about a dozen lights scattered in the hills beyond, including the house across the valley. Off to the south I hear the familiar sound of dogs barking, closer than I expected. In answer, more dogs down in the valley add their howls. They sound like hounds for sure. Because the Park corridor narrowly follows the river, I imagine it's not far to private ground. But so far, no noise from trucks or four-wheelers, even though there's a dirt road in the meadow across the river from camp. But I can hear the gentle *whoosh* of the river below.

In the fading light I walk over to the edge of the bluff one last time tonight to gaze over the river. In the bend of the river just below, I can see the wake from a river otter swimming against the current. As soon as it disappears underwater, another pops up nearby, and together they splash their way to the riverbank. They swim back out into the current, as if playing tag. I smile and watch until I can no longer see them.

Returning to the warm circle of the fire, I'm ready to start supper. I don't have a good way to set up the pot on the fire, so I use the stove. The pot is already hot to the touch, so it shouldn't take long to get it boiling. After pumping the handle on the fuel cylinder, I soon see the blue ring of fire roaring on the stove and warm my hands over it before putting on the pot. I dig out the butter and drop a huge dollop in the pot. I need the calories. I put the lid back on and wait a few minutes till it boils.

The coals of the fire are glowing pleasantly in the light breeze, not unlike the coals of, say, a barbecue. Nearly every thought right now is related to food. I laugh it off and grab another stick for the fire.

The routine of camp is second nature and smoother than ever. Living this simply makes almost any other life seem wildly extravagant. Instead of adjusting a thermostat, I put on more clothing and add more wood to the fire. Instead of turning a knob on a stovetop, I pump the fuel bottle a couple times, twist the throttle till the liquid fuel seeps into the cup, then turn the throttle off and light it. That's my stove. And instead of porcelain toilet in a bathroom, I have a forest full of old mossy logs on which to sit. Some of them even have good views. The woods make good wallpaper.

To me, coming into the woods doesn't bring on some mystical, Thoreau-like spirituality. That's not fair to either the woods or spirituality. I think the joy people find in the outdoors is more of an instinctual return to normality and a break from the complications that our technologically-obsessed society has foisted upon itself. Humans have spent far more time, as a species, as subjects to nature's elements than in large cities, battered by the sounds of sirens, stereos, and televisions with airplanes and helicopters roaring overhead.

There are plenty of people who live like that and enjoy it, but it is still feels like an artificial environment to me. Like an aquarium takes away the wildness of a fish, so the city takes away the wildness of man. And the humanity. There's no place to feel less human than in a crowded city street. It's easier to walk with the herd than to be a free person.

I know: I've lived in big cities, I've been a faceless

member of the crowd. But it never felt right to me, and I hope it never will.

Sitting by the fire sure makes me philosophical. I'm awoken from my thoughts by the rattle of the pot lid, meaning the water's boiling. I add the powdered sauce and macaroni, and in ten minutes I have a huge pot of food.

The stars are shining brightly now, despite the bright light of my campfire. This is the most open site I've camped in since the one overlooking the Little Mulberry Valley a week ago, the night of the fantastic moonrise. A small cloud of pink still sits on the western horizon, turning to purple, and finally, to black. The light from Harrison is shining from behind the mountain, though not as bright as I figured it would be. Somewhere below the eastern horizon, Orion is waiting to emerge and begin his nightly hunt through the galaxy.

Meanwhile, supper's ready and I'm trying hard not to burn my mouth with the hot, cheesy pasta. The warm steam rising up from the pot both smells and feels good. It's tricky, because if I wait till the top layer is cool enough to eat, the rest will be unpleasantly cold. I just have to power through it.

With the warmth of the campfire so comforting, I chide

myself for not building one earlier in the trip. But on the other hand, waiting has made this one that much better. It was worth the cold of the Lewis Prong Valley, Boomer Hollow, Cedar Creek, and last night for this night. Worth it all, in fact: the foot-aches, the back-aches, the leg-aches, sleeping on the ground, not taking a shower for the past eleven days, and missing my girlfriend. All that brought me here for this spectacular evening in the woods.

One thing better than being tucked into bed with a book is sitting beside a fire and reading one. I make short work of my after-supper chores and settle in for one last date with Dostoyevsky. Though I had my doubts initially, I am glad this book has turned out to be as good as it is. It successfully occupied me every evening and many afternoons on this trip, making it worth the weight. Classic literature, indeed.

But as the night wears on, the Karamazov brothers become too much for my tired eyes. The lure of my sleeping bag, barely visible beyond the ring of campfire light, overpowers me. I piss, brush my teeth, and kick some dirt on what's left of the fire. Despite my fatigue, I feel one last surge of excitement run through me. I've made it so far and have just a little more to go.

12

A thin veneer of autumn frost covers the cold, brown ground around my sleeping bag on this last morning. The early light filters through the bare oaks to the east, where from beyond the Ozark Plateau the dawn is moving towards me. I fire up a brimming cup of water for tea, for warmth more than for the caffeine. While packing up camp for the last time I choke down the splintered remnants of the mini wheats. That's one thing I *won't* miss.

  The humidity here in the river corridor seems to sharpen the cold, enough for it to penetrate to the bone. Every the fiery spectacle of dawn does little to warm the air. Nonetheless, the new day brings a fresh round of birdsong to the air, as the winter residents remain. Once I drain my tea I—like the birds—am ready to start again.

Unlike the steep upper reaches of the Buffalo, this area is easier on the legs, with pleasant rolling hills replacing the mountains. The prospect of finishing gives my legs a welcome burst of vigor, while the cold—as always—motivates me to move fast and keep warm. Today there is no hurry, but there is one worry: will my truck be at the end?

As I leave camp, a glance back to the west shows a line of high, gray clouds moving this way. If there's rain with it, it looks like it will be a while. Furthermore, even if it rains, I won't have to camp in it. At least, not if my truck is where I hope it is.

But really, I have nothing to worry about. I have shelter and plenty of food in my pack, and a constant source of clean water off to my left. The walking isn't difficult and I feel good. All I could hope for.

Coming down a hill into a large field, I see a hunter. My hunch that hunting was allowed in the Park was correct: it's one of the few parks that allows it. But this is one of them, and here I am walking around in the early morning in prime deer and elk habitat. I groan at the thought of my orange vest lying beside a log a hundred miles back. But there's nothing I can do about it now.

Plus, I seem to have lost the way. There's an intersection with a horse trail, but the trail soon peters out in the middle of the field. Not where I want to be. I retrace my steps twice, then figure the best option is the road. So I crunch through the frosty green grass along a thin wooded slough. Rounding a slight bend, I find myself at the wrong end of a high-powered rifle and a perturbed hunter.

"You can git killed out here walkin' round like that," he whispers harshly, but not without some truth. I want to argue with him that the responsibility goes both ways and that it's my park, too, but I suppress the urge and apologize to him. I also ask if he knows where the trail goes from here, or if he's seen any trail markers, but he just shrugs me off and heads out into the field. Fair enough. I don't mind putting all the distance I can between me and that rifle.

By now the high clouds have arrived overhead and they cast their dour pallor over the area. Back on the road I see a trail marker down the way, so I head that direction. There's an old house nearby, likely once inhabited by a farming family that took advantage of this naturally fertile bottomland.

A little ways further I cross what I assume to be Calf Creek, which is nothing more than a dry bed full of dirty, rounded stones. The road continues off to the southeast, through the middle of another large field, but the trail splits off to the left and up the side of a low bluff. Before heading into the woods I look around for more hunters or any elk, but see none. A quick motion overhead catches my eye and within a few seconds I can clearly make out a Bald Eagle flying into the west wind. It glides along with barely a flap of its wide wings. A distant gunshot off to the south draws my attention away just long enough for the bird to disappear over a low ridge. I watch for a few more moments, hoping it will circle back with the wind, but after a minute I know it is gone. I turn back to the trail and keep hiking.

Back in the woods I feel out of harm's way, as well as out of the wind. The trail quarters up the bluff in a steady, gentle climb. I'm glad to be back on the trail again and off the road. I sing quietly to myself as I make my way through the trees.

An intersection just ahead gives me two options: take a

left towards the Park Visitor Center, or take a right and stay on the Buffalo River Trail and through an old homestead. I take the latter. This is what I would assume the future route of the OHT would be, but do not know for sure.

A sign at the homestead tells me that this place once belonged to a settler named Sod Collier, as fine a name as I've ever heard. I take a few minutes to look around, admiring the craftsmanship of the buildings, especially the stone-lined well. Like much of the country through which I've passed, this area was quite remote up until about forty years ago, with few neighbors and no electricity. A display up by the park road shows a picture of Mr. and Mrs. Collier looking quite content on their little piece of earth. I can certainly see why: fertile bottomland just down the hill, a mild climate. I wonder what they'd think of this area now, a National Park, with their house a historical landmark.

From here it's about two miles to Highway 65, the official endpoint of my hike. Not the stopping point, though: I'll have to double-back to the visitor center to get to my truck. After the homestead the trail stays well south of the river, with few views through the trees of anything but more trees.

But the excitement continues to build. I even jog for a

few short stretches just to release some of the energy. It's not long before I can hear the roar of the semis gearing down as they descend to the river bridge. I pass a picturesque little stone wall on the left as the trucks get louder and closer. The trail, getting progressively narrower, winds down into a small creekbed and past what looks like an old gauging station. A few steps further and I see a silver streak of metal and plastic flash through the trees. I have reached the highway, and the bridge isn't far.

This is where the trail turns from dirt to pavement. No signs, just overgrown weeds and the detritus of our motorized society. None of the cars on the highway seem to even notice me as I pick my way towards the bridge. The bridge itself is nothing to write home about, just another steel and concrete block hanging over one of America's last free-flowing rivers.

The river itself is quite shallow, the bottom visible through the placid green water. A small limestone bluff, not unlike the one on which I spent last night, looms over the riverbed on the south side. I pause for a few minutes on the middle of bridge, directly over the water. The cars rattle and the trucks rumble just a few feet away, making me thankful for the walled-off walkway.

I figure the best endpoint would be the north side of the bridge, where the future route might very well go. I amble that way, in no hurry at all. I reach the end of the abutment just as a southbound car passes me, so I give them a friendly wave. They don't wave back.

So this is the end: 180 miles on foot across northwest Arkansas. I look around, smile to myself, then head back south across the bridge, back to the bridge, my truck, and the rest of my life. I feel a welcome sense of lightness, as if the entire weight of the journey has been lifted from me. Even my pack feels light, more like a part of me than a mere piece of gear.

Soon I'll find the answer to the big question I've been wondering about all morning: *will my truck be there?* It's the twelfth day since I started, though I don't know if my parents had the time or inclination to get it here. Even from their cabin it's more than a two-hour roundtrip drive to get here, and a drive they may not be keen to do after driving two more hours from their house. But, they also know I was planning on fourteen days or less, and that I can move quickly through the woods.

In the event it's not there, I figure I can make a call from the visitor center and then—of course—start walking. There's a cheap motel a few miles up the road I could walk to until further arrangements can be made. Or I could try hitchhiking into Harrison, then try to catch another ride down Highway 7. Their place is only three miles off of that.

With all that settled, I relax my mind and try to enjoy this last stretch of walking. Passing back along the rock wall, I see a few birds flitter and twitter in the winter gloom and cold. They never fail to cheer me.

The walking is as easy as it's ever been, with just a few minor ups and downs and the always-welcome crunch of leaves under my boots. The trail leads through a section of the campground, which is completely deserted today. Not even the RVers on their way to Branson dared to stop and stay here.

From the campground it's just a short walk up the road to the visitor center. With my truck clearly visible in the parking lot, the scene is a welcome one. As I cross the circle drive, I figure this would be a good spot to take a self-portrait, in front of the Tyler Bend Visitor Center sign. I set my camera on a nearby stone wall and set the timer, then run to the sign.

It takes a few attempts to get a good picture, but there's no one else out here to help me with it.

My truck keys are right where they're supposed to be, so I unlock the doors and throw my pack in the passenger seat. After all we've been through, it seems a little rude to throw it in the back.

Once again, I feel like I've only been away for a weekend or so. But so much has happened since I took those first steps eleven days ago at Lake Fort Smith. It almost feels like a different lifetime. But it also feels like it was just yesterday that I was skinny-dipping in Hurricane Creek, restocking from my cache yesterday morning. It's a strange double-sense of time.

Even with my watch on the whole time, to wake me up, figure out how much daylight is left, or what my hiking pace is, time in a wider sense has little meaning out here, other than day and night. Perhaps because my sense of time, focused on minutes and hours, is so much more narrow than the meaning of the amount of time it took for the Ozark Plateau to rise, then be carved by rivers and creeks. Though I have little idea how long that took, I'll be thankful all my days that in my own brief time, I have had the good fortune to see and experience it.

    To be able to wake up every morning and go for a long walk in the autumn woods is what I wanted to get from this hike.

After a brief foray into the visitor center for a drink of water and a quick chat with the ranger on duty, I load up in my truck and head for my parents' cabin. Just driving through the parking lot, I feel like I'm flying. 25 MPH seems like warp speed. It takes me several miles to get comfortable enough to even approach the speed limit.

    Once I reach Highway 65 I take a left, driving down to the river bridge I recently left. I slowly drive across the bridge, watching till the last possible moment for it to disappear in my mirrors. I'm moving on now.

    A large dog, probably a Redbone, crashes down the embankment on the right side of the highway, directly into my path. Stomping and pumping on the brakes, the tail end of my truck all over the road, I manage to miss the dog. It doesn't appear to have even seen me. I only have a second of relief before I see a Chevy in the oncoming lane. The driver nor the dog see each other. I don't see it, but I hear the collision. In my rearview mirror I see the dog tumble and slide across the highway, like a rag doll. I am horrified. All the joy I felt is gone. My emotions already raw from the finish of my journey, I pull over up the road and cry. I desperately want to get out of my truck and back into the woods. I don't feel comfortable out here.

But I do keep going, back to the cabin. At first, I can barely speak to my parents, who are overjoyed to see me. It takes a while, but I share with them the highlights of my trip. That night, after they leave, I turn off the lights and sip drink after drink as I stare at the fire. At home, but still out of place.

The End.

Epilogue

The Ozark Highlands Trail was conceived as being part of trans-Ozark pathway, an idea that is still expanding to this day. As of this writing, in the winter of 2015-16, the trail is 218 miles of constructed trail and still growing, as any good idea should. I look forward to returning and seeing the new parts of the trail, as well as my favorite places on the original.

Again, I can't emphasize enough how grateful I am to the maintainers of the trail. As a firefighter, I know how hard it is digging and sawing in the woods. Thank you.

Now that you've read this account, I challenge you to put this book down and go for a walk yourself. Life's too short to spend it inside. It's a beautiful world out there. Go experience it. Now.

Resources

Here are some links to some online resources related to the trail, as well as myself.

Ozark Highlands Trail Association and Information, including maps:
http://ozarkhighlandstrail.com/

Ozark Highlands Trail Guidebook:
http://timernst.com/Products/OHT.html

As a native Arkansawyer myself, I also recommend all of the picture books on his site.

Me:
https://mattdunnonline.wordpress.com/

Facebook: https://www.facebook.com/AuthorMattDunn

Instagram: @plantstrongmatt

Twitter: @CatahoulaFan

Made in the USA
Monee, IL
02 March 2020